Angelic

Awakenings

Cover: The angel painting was created by Jill Michelle through the inspiration and artistic intuition from her angels during her second art class. This painting is an excellent expression of how angels can project creativity through people. With angels, possibilities are limitless!

Editor: Heather Embree

Library and Archives Canada Cataloguing in Publication

Service, Jill, author
    Angelic awakenings : notes of an angel reader / Jill Service.

    Includes index.
    Issued in print and electronic formats.
    ISBN 978-0-9948826-0-8 (paperback).--ISBN 978-0-9948826-1-5 (pdf)

        1. Spirituality. I. Title.

BL624.S468 2015   204'.4   C2015-906463-5
                                                 C2015-906464-3

Printed in United States of America

Published by Jill Michelle
www.jillmichelle.ca
First Edition, 2015

Angelic Awakenings

Notes of an Angel Reader

By Jill Michelle

Angelic Awakenings

ACKNOWLEDGEMENTS

I thank Tyler for his encouragement, his insight and for his eagerness to help his computer-challenged mom no matter how busy he was! I am grateful to Spencer for his infectious inspiration and enthusiasm toward this book. I thank Bruce for his unconditional support and for his willingness to share his spiritual wisdom. I am blessed with Jack B. Nimble, my trusty steed who keeps me grounded and focused and relaxed. I am so very grateful for Spirit and the angelic realm, for their motivational driving force and for entrusting me to channel their essential information and messages to those who are ready to listen.

Angelic Awakenings

Table of Contents

Angelic Awakenings

PREFACE

From as young an age as I can remember, I have heard angelic voices speaking to me and have felt the presence of these awesome, highly vibrational beings. When I was in physical danger the angels would guide me towards a safe place. When I was sad they would cheer me up. Sometimes months would go by before I heard from them again. Later in my life I dedicated myself to learning how to communicate with the angels at *my* will, instead of them randomly contacting me. After what seemed like a very long process I was able to do so. My angels gradually became my teachers, and together we explored ways to maintain contact, heighten my clairvoyant abilities, and to help others attain similar goals. My angels guided me almost every step of the way during the writing of this book. They gently but firmly insisted that I organize the book in two parts; the autobiography followed by the companion book and that I include all exercises that will help the readers to advance on their spiritual paths.

About 14 years ago, my angels' presence became more plentiful, and amplified to the point that they were practically shouting at me. I could no longer ignore them. Cultivating my relationship with the angels was strenuous and time consuming. Many days I was frustrated to the point of relinquishing my goal of becoming highly clairaudient, but they always gently encouraged me to propel myself forward. I soon realized that I had been given a distinct and valuable gift that, if enhanced and perfected, could potentially produce beneficial results for others as well as for myself. This aptitude of intuitive revelation surfaced after an invisible rescuer saved me from a life-threatening equestrian accident. This life-changing event spurred me on to my journey of self-discovery, and to seek out and connect to universal wisdom and light.

My celestial friends urged me to spend hours walking through forests of divine nature, absorbing the profound grounding energy that was essential for the advancement of my soul purpose. There were no questions I could ask that the angels could not answer, even while contemplating all aspects of life throughout the Earth and the Universe. It was so humbling to be such a small speck in the vastness of the universe and yet knowing that everyone was important and their missions were vital to the universal plan. I spent many hours in silent meditation expanding my communication abilities, awareness and knowledge. I continually cleared myself of negativity and filled myself with love-light, guided by methods that the angels revealed to me. From the depths of despair and overwhelming challenges, my life became healthy, conscious, compassionate, and limitless. My angels comforted me and provided relief from emotional turmoil by explaining to me the reasons inherent to any particular situation. When I was lost and needed direction to find my way, these divine beings would escort me out of the maze of an unknown forest or lead me through the labyrinth-like congestion of city streets until I was in familiar territory. They bestowed upon me information and knowledge that cleared my confusion in numerous life circumstances, sometimes by seeing through other people's eyes or by walking in their shoes.

My angels brought me peace and tranquillity when I needed it most, often by revealing the serenity of Mother Earth through guided visits to breath-taking vistas of high altitudes, placid lakes, cascading rivers, quiet forest trails and peaceful green meadows. They showed me upcoming events and how to address them to achieve the best possible outcome for all. The angelic realm helped me to process what seemed to be disastrous experiences, and to learn from them, and be harmonious with them.

I know they are always present and accompany me every moment of my life. They help me to see and know that everyone has similar celestial beings constantly surrounding them with intense love. They are patiently waiting for us to open our hearts and tap into their awe-inspiring godly energy. Eventually, when I was able to call on the divine ones at will and trust that I was receiving their messages and suggestions clearly, my life changed forever.

About six years after I started my spiritual journey, I was directed to begin work as an angel reader. Ultimately I was guided to help people generate peace, love and happiness into their lives through Intuitive Life Coaching. During the channelling sessions I share with my clients, the angels shower us with profound highly vibrational energy. I am so grateful and honoured that I am able to be a part of this intense and demonstrative offering of unconditional love that the light beings project to all of humanity.

My friends and clients consistently expressed their desire for me to write a book about my life and ability to do intuitive work so they could understand and grow from my account. They think I have outstanding gifts or talents, but I truly know that all people have intuitive abilities and are able to develop their skills and capabilities just as I have. We are all born with various gifts such as the abilities to intellectualize, sing, dance, organize, play an instrument, act, paint, sculpt, build, create and so on. To realize my gifts it was a matter of clearing away blockages and learning how to listen to the subtle energies the universe offers.

I have recollected many of the messages and events in my life. This book may be read purely for curiosity, or it could be used as a learning tool to further your own journey of enlightenment. My aspiration is that this information gives you insight into your own purpose for being on Earth at this time of monumental change. It has taken me a long time to achieve what I have so far. My purpose is to help you to advance on your spiritual path in a shorter time span than otherwise might be attainable, and to guide you more quickly through obstacles and completely avoid hindrances that slowed me down when I started.

I cannot express enough how my interaction with angels and light beings has brought me to an unequivocal state of peace. I trust that by following the insights this book offers, you too will generate more love, peace and happiness into your life.

My journey to enlightenment began innocently as I searched for unconditional love and universal truth. Only then did the truth of life start to become clearer in increasing ways. I invite you to join me as I recount my journey in the hopes that it will inspire you to expand your spiritual horizons and walk or rather run along your own path of enlightenment, shining your luminous soul-light upon all humanity.

INTRODUCTION

There comes a time in everyone's life when they realize or at least hope that there is more to life than physical existence; that the Spirit world and Nirvana or Heaven really do exist. That their soul will go on to a more beautiful place, not just vanish into nothingness. This desire may occur due to apprehension at the end of one's life, or when a loved one has passed away or when there is no other option than to face the inevitable. Blessed are those who elect unprovoked to venture forth on their spiritual path through faith and optimism.

Following the direction this book offers will generate momentum and interest in revealing the Truth that only genuine spirituality presents. Life can offer enjoyment to the fullest for all the rest of your days. This is where trust and faith come in. Trust that you and your Higher Power have created a life fitting for your soul's perfect journey. Have faith that you will choose the highest path, as we are all created by our Higher Power's perfect creative ability. It is neither possible nor necessary for you to understand everything in this world. When you demonstrate your intent to fulfil your soul purpose, information from many sources will be displayed to you including; nudges from your angels and guides, and from broad-based synchronicities. Then the opening up of light pathways for your soul will follow. As you climb the ladder of enlightenment these rays of light become much more prevalent and obvious and you will be given the innate knowledge of how to proceed.

What is enlightenment? It is a spiritual revelation or deep insight into the meaning and purpose of all things. It is communication with and understanding of and ultimately becoming one with your Higher Power. It is a changed consciousness where everything is perceived as Oneness and Unity. The journey to en*light*enment is simple: absorb the light. Light is love. Release the dark. Darkness is fear. Living in the light *is* living in the state of Love. Living in the dark *is* living in the state of fear.

Duality on Earth demonstrates that there are only two general emotions: love and fear. Everything falls under these two categories. Some people may relate this to their concept of good versus evil. Examples of love: light, positivity, joy, peace, kindness, sharing, giving, helping, respect, safety, trust, security, freedom, faith, friendliness, openness, service to others, and anything that comes from a place of love. Conversely fear includes: darkness, negativity, greed, control, sadness, insecurity, anxiety, despair, boastfulness, hate, jealousy, anger, racism, nastiness, prejudice, irritability, close mindedness, selfishness, hoarding, meanness, stealing, destruction, abuse, war and so on. Note that light and dark refers to the inner state of being and never anything whatsoever to do with a person's skin, hair or eye colour, which is completely irrelevant.

You can learn the nuts and bolts here, but the true process of your enlightenment belongs to you. You must take charge of your journey and continuously ask the right questions in order to receive the perfect answers. Doing this will continually propel you higher on your path and eventually you will reach the state of enlightenment.

These chapters delve into information and methods to bring forth necessary components of achieving a more illuminated existence. For example: releasing negativity, enhancing positivity, replenishing with light, developing forgiveness and non-judgment for self and others, accepting what is, residing in the soul space, cultivating gratefulness which allows for receiving, manifesting abundance, non-attachment and freedom to be the true you, invoking humility, and improving relationships are some of the areas that will be covered.

Channellings were bestowed upon me with the intention that they be included in this book. They are offered as an insight to benefit and advance the reader on the journey to become one with Creator and all creation.

Book One is an autobiography, which explains the beginnings of my connection with the angelic realm. Included are stories from my childhood which pertain to my angels and guardian angels, and the wonderful intuition that I received from them. I have recounted events throughout my adult life that helped me learn to trust and to communicate with my angels.

Book Two is about how specific intuitive messages and instructions improved my life through increased love and connection to my Higher Power and the Universe. This information is delivered in such a way that it can be read for enjoyment and information, or can be studied for personal use toward your own path of enlightenment. Each chapter includes exercises that increase understanding of how that particular concept relates to you personally. If you do the exercises with intention, you will move higher on your soul path.

As you read through these pages, you will absorb what is written according to your perspective in the present moment. As you learn to release negativity and absorb light, your perspective will change. What you learn from this book today will be different from what you will learn if you reread this book a year from now, or 3 years from now. As you climb the ladder of enlightenment, your perspective progressively changes to reflect life according to Universal Truth.

The entire book was written from my perspective of Universal Truth and how it relates to me and my life. In addition to conversations, the angels often communicate to me through light, vibrations, and feelings. I have done my best to use words that describe the closest interpretation of these energies. I have included the generic terms Higher Power and Spirit throughout the book. To me, Higher Power is God, and is used to denote the omnipresent highest power in this Universe. Divine Mother is the nurturing feminine aspect of God. Spirit is the Holy Spirit, the aspect of God who is the go-between Heaven and Earth. He fulfils God's will and brings light energy to Earth and humanity. Jesus is the aspect of God who performs miracles, healings and much more. Angels are sparks of God, many of whom are eternally devoted to specific souls. They do His work and spread His messages to their charges and to the entire world. Together these beings promote oneness with Creator or All There Is.

Generic terms were used specifically so that, you are able to infuse whomever *you* believe in more easily into these expressions. My desire is for you to be comfortable with the wording and therefore able to absorb the entirety of the concepts, and advance along your path of illumination.

BOOK ONE

AUTOBIOGRAPHY

CHAPTER 1

THE EARLY YEARS

I have many recollections of times in my early life of what I much later realized were angelic voices helping and guiding me. As a child I heard a 'guiding voice', especially when playing hide and seek: "Jill hide here," leading me to stand behind a tree. "You'll be safe here from being caught" was the message. My reaction of course was: "Are you kidding? I'm almost in plain view of the seeker." Time and time again, the seeker would be unable to detect me in my often so obvious hiding place. The other children hiding would often exclaim that they could not believe that I was not found! I never got caught when I listened to that intelligent inner voice. When I ignored the voice and found a great hiding spot which I thought would be difficult for the seeker to discover, I was always one of the first ones to be found. The guiding voice would always very politely and patiently encourage me to follow its advice. My celestial guides were completely without any desire to win, so they were not helping me in that regard. They were showing me through example that it was important for me to listen and follow their advice. In so doing, I would be safe.

There were repeated similar scenarios throughout my childhood. I would be guided away from a certain area in a lake where shortly afterward someone who ventured there fell into a hole through the rock bottom, twisting an ankle. I was likewise escorted away from a waterfall where another person was soon cut by a treacherous sharp piece of glass. Many times I was led away from potentially dangerous people and places.

I remember skipping home from grade school, seemingly alone to onlookers, listening and laughing out loud at the joyful and funny stories my guides told me. People would look at me as they passed by in their cars, or on their bikes, I'm sure they were wondering what I could possibly be laughing about. I often had the company and camaraderie of my guides and their input. They would comfort me in times of anxiety, and cheer me up in times of sadness, lead me away from danger and bring my attention to anything that would give me a joyful laugh. I was never alone and always felt so happy in the company of my celestial guides.

I was frequently listening to several of my guide's voices at a time, hence when my mother was added as one more voice, I didn't give my full attention to her. She came to the conclusion that I was "clueless" and labelled me so. I know she was being the best mom she could be by directing attention to my in-attention, but unfortunately this along with other childhood experiences was detrimental to my self-esteem which remained low for many years.

I was ten years old when I asked my mom if everyone had this helpful voice inside them. She replied, "Oh yes dear, run along and play." I was quite happy to have been told that the voices were normal. It wasn't until considerably later in my life, that I realized that this was a standard answer to pretty much any mystical question I asked my mom. I continually asked my friends how they could have possibly ignored their inner voices especially when they walked directly into troublesome situations. Invariably they would look at me with a blank look on their face. I finally arrived at the conclusion that not everyone had developed the ability to listen to their inner guidance system... yet. I became increasingly aware that these wise voices I listened to were not of my making. They had information that I could not have possibly known. It was much later in my life that I realized this communication was from a higher intelligence which I was privy to. I eventually understood that the voices were from my Guardian Angels, Teaching Angels and other helpful Light Beings who were interconnecting with me.

Numerous times during my childhood I was given the opportunity to see incidents that most people do not experience. One of these occasions was when I was 11 years old. I was vacationing at my Grandparent's cottage. We were all gathered at the kitchen table having dinner, and to everyone's surprise there came a knock at the door. This was an extremely rare occurrence. My mother peeked through the window to see a man who was known notoriously for his habit of glue-sniffing. She yelled through the closed door: "Go away, there's nothing for you here." Mom immediately instructed my oldest sister to hide, and she promptly ran out of the kitchen and hid in the bedroom. The man at the door lived on the island not far away. Many of the cottagers were afraid of him, imagining that he would harm them or worse. There would often be phone calls from neighbours down the beach warning us that the "glue sniffer" was coming our way and to take refuge. We would retreat into the cottage for a while, spying out the windows to make sure he had passed by and we would be safe. The following summer I saw him limping through the bush a stone's throw from where I was playing. He did not see me, or at least was oblivious to my presence. This was the first time I had seen him. I knew instantly from deep within that he would not hurt me or anyone else. That was not even part of his consciousness. I had a heart-felt feeling of compassion for this unusual man. Many years later, after his death, we learned from a policeman who had known him that he was a kind and gentle man; he had never harmed anyone. He was only trying to cope with his own problems through his insatiable addiction.

Another incident where I was being guided was when I was 12 years old, and I was at the Canadian National Exhibition with a friend. During the course of the day, we decided to go to the Coliseum which was at the other end of the fair. My friend thought taking a short cut through a path less travelled would get us to our destination faster. She headed down a pathway that led to an area where the carnival men had erected their tents. I had counsel from the angels to not go down that alleyway. I cautioned her that it was not a safe path to take, but she ran ahead of me, cheekily disregarding my warning. With a heavy anxious feeling in my gut, I followed her, not wanting to lose her in the crowded fair. Before long I saw a belligerent man accosting her and taunting her with vulgar overtones. Breathlessly, I caught up with her just as another taller man exited his tent and confronted the offensive man. Grateful for the distraction of the larger man, we quickly made our escape. These and other incidents created within me trust and faith that I would be safe, if I listened carefully and followed the advice of the angels.

During my early teens, a build-up of negative energies from life circumstances gathered within me. I was a sensitive child and even the realization that my parents were not the mythical beings I had once been enamoured with added to the other common events that happened during maturation. It was an upsetting time for me. I developed anxiety and started to live in fear, which created a static cloud of negativity that encompassed me. This blocked the delicate angelic vibrations from penetrating my consciousness. My telepathic communication with the angels became mute and I became distanced from my angels. Many people have great angel communication as youngsters, and then let it go as they grow and step away from the inner knowing they were born with, and become more entwined with the third dimensional life on Earth, as I did.

As with all people, my angels remained constantly by my side, and looked out for my safety. They interceded with help, but only when it was in my soul path's best interest to do so. They refrained from playful interaction with me throughout the course of my days. Very soon I lost all memory, knowledge, and understanding of the angelic realm. My new life without the angels became the norm for me. The communication channel changed; intuition was solely transmitted to me through gut feelings or inner knowing instead of auditory and extrasensory messages. Many years later I learned how to release the fear from my inner child who was associated with those upsetting childhood incidents. Ultimately, I started hearing the joyful angelic voices again. They became progressively louder and more numerous. I guess we had a lot of catching up to do!

I was born and raised in a mainstream suburban family north of Toronto, Ontario with my parents and three sisters. We had one dog and two cats. My two older sisters and I rode horses ever since we were youngsters. As a family we down-hill skied in the winter at Blue Mountain, where after skiing my sisters and I would play outside in the snow with our dog Susie, making snow forts and tunnels through the snowbanks. We visited my grandparent's cottage on Georgian Bay in the summer, which nurtured my love for beaches, sun, lakes, swimming, water-skiing and boating. I have fond memories of my family travelling to Europe, western Canada, and the United States for summer and winter vacations.

After high school at my dad's insistence, I attended University for one year, and much to his chagrin I quit. Completely enamoured with the idea of becoming a health care practitioner, I applied for and completed the course at a Community College. I have worked as a health care practitioner for over thirty years, and have worked part-time at the same office for twenty years. I enjoy working with my friendly and supportive co-workers, and appreciate all the meaningful relationships with my clients/patients.

I was married to my high school sweetheart at the age of 23. We have two magnificent boys named Tyler and Spencer. I was a proud hockey mom and enthusiastically attended my boys' sports meets and school performances. They have now grown up to be brilliant and amazing men. Through the years we rescued two cats named Dickens and Bobby, and a horse named Jack, and we acquired a horse named Toby and a wire coated dachshund named Heidi, who thought she was human. Sadly but amicably, our 30 year marriage ended in divorce.

I joyfully sang in the barbershop Sweet Adelines International Orangeville Chorus for six years. I don't read music, so I learned my baritone part by persistently listening and singing along with a cassette tape while driving the car. My boys were probably among the few children in the world who knew the baritone part for all the Sweet Adelines songs!

I bravely joined Toastmaster's International several years ago, which has helped me enormously to write and perform presentations and workshops.

I ride horses on the weekends with my friends, and love swimming, hiking, biking, downhill skiing, and travelling.

I enjoy being with my friends and family. I too experience my dreams, ambitions, defeats and wins.

For many years I led an ordinary and conventional life. After my shocking spiritual awakening, I resisted the fact that I had an aptitude for intuition: I was in denial. I spent a lot of time telling the angels that they had the wrong person; that I was way too normal to have this unusual perceptive ability. I didn't tell any of my friends or family about my intuitive gifts. I was worried that they would think I was peculiar. I'd heard stories about people who heard voices in their heads being locked away, so I was concerned about expressing my predicament to anyone. I knew I was completely sane, in fact I felt saner than the large majority of people, but was not convinced that others would agree. I did not yet comprehend the significance of intuition, or the fullness of my circumstance. I had no one to confide in or to explore the concept with. It was a difficult and challenging existence. I hesitantly asked the angels to give the gift to someone else instead. They left me alone for a while, but eventually returned and wisely brought me someone who helped immensely. I am very grateful for my friendship with Lesley Young, my first spiritual friend. She helped me understand my intuitive perception, and encouraged me to hone my skills. She loaned me books about meditation and angels, and hosted two spiritual workshops that I attended. She introduced me to other spiritual people, and most importantly to my mentor. I finally appreciated and accepted my gift and ran with it. I am a normal everyday person who happens to have an intuitive aptitude.

Looking back at my teenage years; when I was 16, I rode my first horse Sonatina, down the road a couple of miles to a Horse Club meeting. I joined a friend of mine who boarded her horse along the same road and we arrived at the meeting facility together. I had not yet consistently jumped a horse successfully at that time, and was quite fearful of repeating my all too frequent failure of falling off. There were twenty students on their horses participating while two instructors called out the directives. After a short warm up, we were instructed to drop the reins and stirrups and stretch our arms out to the sides as far as we could, close our eyes, and canter our horses up to and over a two foot jump. Before long that jump was raised a few times, after which more jumps were added to the line. Needless to say, I was not impressed with this seemingly dangerous challenge. However with a lot of encouragement, from the rest of the riders in the class, the cautious riders including myself finally did the exercise to the satisfaction of the instructors. In retrospect, it was probably one of the best riding lessons I ever had. I was finally and gratefully aware of how, when balanced properly, my legs alone were sufficient to keep me in the saddle. Once I returned to having stirrups, reins, and open eyes, the prospect of jumping seemed much easier and more in my comfort zone. Learning that necessary lesson early in my riding days helped my future work in training and showing horses.

Shortly after the lesson my friend and I were in the barn, munching on some treats when a man approached us. He tried to befriend us and invited us to board our horses there at the facility that he ran. I had an uneasy feeling that kept growing steadily until it was screaming at me, and I could no longer ignore it. I felt that I had to get away from that man as fast as I could and to stay away from him. I started to feel very panicky with a sense that my safety depended on me leaving instantly. I immediately gestured to my friend that we were leaving straight away. We never went back.

I occasionally wondered for what purpose that incident occurred. A couple of years later I read an article in the newspaper stating that the same man who we met that day was charged with assaulting young women at his barn. This was a big lesson to me. I needed to respect and honour my intuitive warnings for safety's sake and to follow them meticulously; exiting a given situation with haste when my gut advised me to.

I'm sure that my angels guided my beliefs around God. My father loved going to church and insisted that my mother and sisters and I should go with him. My mother attended often, but was not as fond of church as my dad was. Occasionally she came up with an excuse as to why she would not attend on a given Sunday. Before we left home, she would take us aside and remind us to nudge my father if he fell asleep. My father would invariably be snoozing by the early stage of the sermon. The sister who was seated next to him had the task of elbowing him gently, so he wouldn't be startled awake making an embarrassingly loud snort.

The minister was of Irish descent and had Calvinistic tendencies. He would preach hell and damnation and that we were all sinners during his interminably long and uncomfortable sermons. I could not fathom a God who was unloving and unkind as this minister strongly advocated. His religious God did not fit into my inner knowing. I became increasingly more distanced from the church and less inclined to follow religious beliefs. I'm sure this is why the notion of kind and loving angels reached me with welcoming arms, as I had refrained from taking in the minister's opposing religious beliefs.

I have personally experienced the angels saving lives. One time my boyfriend and I were riding on the top bunk of a motor home, peering through the window. His mom was driving into a gas station but had unfortunately missed the driveway. The motor home was advancing directly toward the wide deep ditch directly ahead. We saw the left tire was still barely on the edge of the driveway, but the right tire and three quarters of the vehicle was moving directly for the ditch. Viewing from our high perch, we knew we were headed for certain death. Remarkably the motor home magically skirted over the top of the gully! It was as if there was an imaginary bridge allowing us safe passage. We stared at each other in astonishment as our shock turned into relief. As soon as the vehicle stopped, we ran to the ditch, wondering if we had been mistaken. We clearly saw a five foot ditch with no bridge overtop, and nothing for the wheel of the motor home to traverse. I'm sure it was our angels protecting us from serious injury or death. I knew deep within that it was a supernatural occurrence and I thanked my guardian angel. Several years before this incident, my aunt had informed me that she believed that everyone had guardian angels and they in turn had the ability to save the person they were connected to. I suddenly and overwhelmingly believed that she was right.

Many people have similar instances where their angels have guarded them from danger. It's common for people to discount or ignore the help their angels give them if they are not aware of anything beyond the physical third dimension. Thanking angels is appropriate and respectful in situations where they have been of assistance.

When my youngest son, Spencer, was five months old he was diagnosed with asthma. By the time he was seven months, he had been plagued by consecutive bouts of asthma. One episode was especially frightening, as the attending physician at The Hospital for Sick Children in Toronto, told me he could die in the night. I was told to stay near him at all times so I could hear if he stopped breathing. I was consumed with worry and so afraid I would fall asleep, because I was exhausted from inadequate sleep since his birth. I was sitting in Spencer's room in a rocking chair cradling his limp little body in my arms as he slept. I prayed with huge intent, that my baby would recover from asthma, and that he would become fully healthy.

Suddenly I felt an extremely powerful presence pass through us from front to back. It felt as if I was being raised up by an invisible energy form. It came with a very strong message that my son would become completely healthy and he would outgrow asthma by the time he was five years old. It was such an all-encompassing experience of the sort that I had never felt before. The message was so overwhelming and persuasive that I had no doubt that it was true. I put my baby in his crib, returned to my room and went to sleep. I slumbered deeply and soundly for the first time in many months.

Over the next few days I pondered frequently about this occurrence. I wanted to know who had aided me in my time of need. I thought in the back of my mind, could it possibly have been Jesus who had come to me and answered my prayers? This was quite a quandary for me as at the time I did not have much faith in religion. The presence that had shown itself to me had such a high resolution of love energy that I knew it was very powerful and was of the highest authority. Spencer did recover completely from asthma by the time he was five years old.

A similar thing happened about seven years later when I received another equally powerful message. My beloved horse Toby had become ill at about 2:00 pm. The local veterinarian and I monitored him and he seemed to be improving at times. Around 11:30 pm he took a serious turn for the worse.

The veterinarian diagnosed Toby with a severe case of colic, which can be life-threatening to a horse, and she suggested I take him for further testing. At 12:30 am, a new friend of mine, Marie-Helen, trailered him to the local Guelph Equine Hospital.

Immediately upon our arrival at the hospital, we were ushered into the clinical examination room and three vets inspected him. They were unable to identify the specifics of Toby's colic from the physical exam they had performed. The vets needed to carry out exploratory surgery to gather more information for an accurate diagnosis and solution. They offered to put him on the operating table and either continue with the operation if he was saveable, or put him to sleep if they thought he was not. The other alternative was to observe him and see if he got better on his own. They required a quick decision from me. It was a lot of money for me at the time and I was reluctant to put my family through a large expenditure. I loved Toby very much and was exceedingly conflicted as to how to proceed. It was 3:00 am and I was exhausted.

At that time in my life I only asked for help from God when I was totally desperate, so I prayed for Him to help me decide. There was one persistent vet who was insisting that I make a quick decision and would not leave me alone. Trying to get some space away from this distraction and to think clearly, I walked quite a long way down a hallway to a drinking fountain, hoping he would not follow me. While I was drinking, to my utter surprise I received a very loud and powerful, love-filled message: "Don't operate." It was so loud I thought that the vet, who actually had followed me down the hall, would have heard it. Apparently he did not. I told him of my decision to not operate. Until that time I had not received any messages so loud and commanding; I immediately decided to follow the instruction. I took Toby back to his designated stall in full confidence that he would recover fully without human interference. A short time later he took a turn for the worse and the only humane option, was to end his life.

I didn't understand this at all. I thought that because the message had come from such a loving place, that Toby would recover and the two of us would be heading home soon. I was very confused and upset. I was very angry with myself for acting on the advice from the voice at the fountain, feeling I had made a grave error and that if I had opted for the operation Toby would have lived.

Five days later, I got a phone call from the veterinary hospital. The autopsy on Toby had been completed and the veterinarian read the charted results to me. Once I heard the results of the autopsy, I understood the message at the fountain. Toby had the rarest type of colic; a diaphragmatic hernia. It was inoperable.

I realized the voice in the fountain had been correct. Receiving the message through my emotionally charged perspective of wanting Toby to live a long and healthy life was the reason why I assumed that he would recover completely. The reality was that I would have been putting undue stress on Toby by granting the authority to do the exploratory surgery. I would also have caused unnecessary financial distress on my family for no purpose, as Toby's condition was fatal.

About 12 years ago, I was having a riding lesson on a friend's horse jumping over fences to prepare for an upcoming show. The riding ring had just been harrowed and one of the jumps had not been returned to its proper place. Unfortunately neither the instructor nor I noticed this. As I cantered the horse into a combination of jumps, I realized too late that there was no possible way for us to avoid an accident. The horse cleared the first jump and landed with her front feet right at the base of the next jump. She was travelling at a fast canter with no possible chance of stopping. She utterly crashed through the second jump; her legs leaped up under the poles and sent them flying in front of my face as her hind legs became entangled in the remaining poles. I knew we were both in big trouble. I was catapulted forward out of the saddle, through the air, landing hard in the sand on my front. My breath was squashed out of my lungs; my arms were pinned underneath my compromised and immobile body. I lay prone in the sand waiting for her to crush me. I knew from the way she had staggered through the fence that she would end up falling on top of me.

Precisely at that moment, I felt a powerful invisible force pulling me ahead about four feet, over the sand like a hovercraft, freeing my arms and filling my lungs with precious air. Just then, my horse came crashing down, her full weight landing below my body. Her chest rolled onto my thighs. Her head and neck were flailing over my back, her front legs clawing the sand in front of my face, spraying me. I could feel the heat from her panicky breath warming the hairs on the back of my neck. Those few seconds seemed to last for an hour. She finally found her footing and scrambled to her feet. As I rose to my feet I did a mental scan of my body. I was sore and bruised, but not broken anywhere. I started to scoop away the sand from my eyes, ears, nose, and spat out as much as I could from my mouth. All I could think of was "What the heck just happened here?" Had I not been pulled forward, I would certainly have been crushed by the weight of the 1200 pound horse crashing down on me. The instructor's view was obstructed by fences so she was unable to see the accident from her vantage point in the middle of the riding ring. She was unaware that I was rescued by some imperceptible power. I was alone to ponder on what had actually happened.

At first I was very angry with myself that I had not noticed that the jumps were in a dangerous location in the ring that day. I was furious with the whole situation and mostly that the horse was hurt and may possibly never jump again. My inner voice said it was important that this happened, and that I would understand later. Those words haunted me for a long time.

I couldn't get that incident out of my head. I contemplated it twenty four-seven. Day in, day out I kept replaying the scene in my head trying to understand it. I told a new friend about the occurrence and she told me of a psychic/angel reader named Krystal who she trusted and believed in. I had never been to, or even thought of going to a psychic before, but I had the gut feeling that this woman would have some important answers for me.

During my visit with the angel reader, she told me that it was my guardian angel who had pulled me forward above the sand out of harm's way. She said it was not my time to die, and I was not to live a life with a maimed body. Even as she was speaking, I felt deep within me that what she was saying was true. It was my first experience with what I now refer to as confirmation goose bumps; the tingly feeling throughout my body accompanied with raised bumps on my arms and legs. I experience this when I know deep within that what I am hearing is true. I knew on some level that I was saved by my guardian angel all along, but it was helpful for me to have Krystal's confirmation for my conscious mind. She explained that guardian angels often save their person, but the person frequently denies that the incident happened and suppresses knowledge of the situation. Sometimes the angels scatter what she described as a sort of 'fairy dust' so the person forgets the details. This happens when the person is not ready to accept that there is a spiritual dimension. She stated that I was ready to learn the lessons that went along with the rescue and therefore had full memory of the divine intervention.

For a few months leading up to this appointment, I was hearing so many voices that it was akin to a party going on in my head all the time. It was virtually impossible to concentrate fully on anything, to think clearly, or to sleep at night. I was somewhat concerned for my sanity. I asked Krystal for clarity on that issue. She laughed as she replied that I had so many angels around my head that I'd have to be deaf to not hear them. She revealed that if I learned how to listen to them clearly, I could do angel readings too! I decided immediately to work toward that goal. The angel reader taught me how to listen to my angels one by one; essentially to line them up in order, with the angels who had the most important messages first. I was relieved and peaceful after the reading, and determined to explore the prospect of my future as an angel reader.

The techniques that Krystal taught me improved my focus and helped me eventually to hone in on specific vibratory frequencies that enabled me to do readings for clients. I became proficient at gaining necessary information from the angels so that I could learn how to be more deeply connected to the spiritual realm. Soon they became my teachers in every aspect of life. I was able to learn life lessons from my own existence and the lives of other people around me.

Angels would often tell me wise and interesting reports and I came to realize they possessed extremely high intelligence. I consequently developed the hunger for wisdom and asked multitudes of questions. I listened to these intelligent voices with intent to absorb all that I could.

So many times I have been asked to trust. I will get messages to do something that I would normally be opposed to, and I am to trust that spirit will keep me safe as I am guided through a certain lesson. Sometimes this information comes through a meditation and sometimes it is physical action I am asked to do. The question asked of me is always: "Do you trust us?" At first I answered with a very hesitant "Yes, I think so, (I hope so)", and very soon I discovered that I was always safe through the trial that ensued. This furthered my faith that angels were availing themselves to me for the purpose of spiritual education and that they would always take good care of me. They taught me the information I am sharing in this book and they are still educating me every day.

CHAPTER 2

THE POWER OF VISUALIZATION

I learned early on that visualization can be used for manifesting what I want into my life. It can be used to decrease unwanted thinking and behaviour, and increase the thinking and behaviour I do want. Dr. M. Maltz, author of the book *"Psycho Cybernetics"* discovered that:

"Change is brought about by experience. Experiencing is the same to the subconscious mind as imagining. The subconscious mind does not know the difference between real and unreal. It accepts what you feed it."

Dr. Maltz performed some experiments and research to successfully prove his theory. I have used visualization for a long time and it really works. If I have a potentially stressful situation coming up, I visualize going through that event filled with powerful and brave energy. I have used this for overcoming fear of public speaking, sport competitions especially after a bad injury, driving confidently again after a bad accident, job interviews and more. Visualization is only one of many ways that meditation can be used to enhance body mind and spirit.

I discovered the valuable influence of visualization through desperation. After I had crash landed on the far side of the stadium jump explained earlier, I became very leery of getting on a horse again, never mind jumping. The unfortunate accident happened only two weeks before a year-end championship show for which I had qualified two horses and very much wanted to participate in. The owner of the horses had already paid my entries for the show and we both had high expectations of me. I was too embarrassed and too responsible to decline the offer to show the remaining healthy horse. I was at a loss as to what to do next.

I talked to a friend of mine who was a very experienced and competitive equestrian. She had previously mentioned to me that she had crashed a few years ago and had become too afraid to jump. I broached the subject with her again, to hopefully find new insight and a quick cure. She explained that it took about a year for her to regain her confidence. She started with walking her horse over poles on the ground and very gradually worked her way up to three foot jumps by increasing the height of the poles by three inches at a time. It took her about six months before she was going over small jumps, and a full year for her to regain her composure over fences at the height from which she had fallen. I realized I only had about 10 days to overcome my fear, as I needed to practice jumping with the horse at least a couple of days before the show.

I had to accomplish in a few days what she had done in one year. My intuition kept nudging me and telling me there was a way. I searched for an answer. I remembered reading about Dr. Maltz who had done research on visualization with a basketball team. He had divided the team into three groups. The first group practiced as usual. The second group visualized their practice sessions only. The third group did nothing. At the end of the specified time, the team was tested and the results were that the group that did nothing had lessened their abilities. The group that had practiced normally had improved slightly and the group that had visualized was by far the most improved.

Armed with this information I embarked on my first effort to visualize. I devoted as much time as possible to this new endeavour. First I started with imagining myself on the horse cantering toward a jump. To my surprise, I quickly became so frightened that I catapulted right out of the visualization and came back to full consciousness instantaneously. It felt so real; as if I was actually on the horse! When I visualized, my mind created a strong simulation to the actual act. My gut became wrenched with fear, and my body perspired. I realized I had to start gently with baby steps just so I could remain in the meditative state.

The strong realization dawned on me that this method would work but time was of the essence. Remembering what my friend had told me of her progress, I started visualizing myself on the horse walking over the pole on the ground. Once I was calm about that, I raised the jump to three inches off the ground, then six, then nine inches and higher. I envisioned gradually increasing the size of the jump to the three feet three inches; the height I would be required to do in the show. I trotted over it and finally cantered over it. I was so thrilled to get this far. I began visualizing two jumps in a row, then three and four. Eventually I was able to canter a whole stadium course of twelve jumps in my mind and feel very comfortable and confident with it.

This whole process took me about a week to accomplish. It was time to put the test to reality. I arranged with the owner to ride the horse and I went to the barn. As I worked around the horse and saddled her up, I felt perfectly at ease. I mounted, and started exercising her. We walked, trotted and cantered. I looked at the jumps and decided to proceed with the task that I had been working on so intently for the last week. I trotted her to the first jump, then cantered over the next few. It was as if I had neither fallen nor experienced any anxiety about riding at all. I felt totally secure and confident jumping! We finished by cantering a twelve jump stadium course for real. The owner of the horse was very impressed and said that if it had been her who had undergone such a bad fall, that she probably would never have jumped again. I assured her that it was all in a week's work. She nodded and half smiled, unaware of what I was referring to. It was a huge revelation for me to think of the realm of possibilities that could be accomplished with visualization. The show day arrived and I rode confidently over all the jumps. The owner of the horse was almost as happy as I was and the day was a success.

I called on my visualization technique a few years later when I was asked to do a workshop. I immediately and excitedly accepted, thinking I would be giving it to only a few people. A month later the venue had been secured; I found out that I would be speaking to a group of 120 people, probably split into two groups. This completely blew my mind. I had been totally paranoid of public speaking ever since I was a child, and was among those who would rather have died than speak in front of an audience. A couple of years previously, my intuition had strongly dictated to me that I needed to learn how to speak in public. Because of this I had taken some workshops on public speaking so I was familiar with how to create an effective and interesting presentation. I had spoken a few times in front of 15 familiar people, but my fear was still very prevalent. My anxiety due to the large scope of the upcoming workshop kept me from sleeping at night and I had difficulty focusing on my daily tasks. Just thinking about the workshop, caused me a very heavy feeling in my chest, a knot in my abdomen and I would break into a sweat. It was more the number of people who would be listening than the content that I was worried about. I decided to visualize since that had worked well for the show jumping. I resolved to design a strategy to prepare myself in case I had to speak in front of one hundred people all at once. I decided to imagine myself going through the following steps in front of twenty people and work my way up from there.

I started with imagining that I was watching someone else doing a speech while I was in the audience. After a few times when I felt comfortable, I visualized myself on stage standing about ten feet away from the speaker, observing her and the audience as she spoke. I looked at the crowd and in time became relaxed. Next I envisioned the speaker asking me a question. I looked at the audience as I answered bravely. I became a bit more confident. I moved closer to the speaker's side. I kept answering questions facing the crowd until that became comfortable and easy. Next I saw the speaker ask me to come to the microphone. I said a line or two into the mic and then stepped back again. This interplay continued until I could speak a few lines at the microphone without feeling stressed. I then pretended to be the person who was speaking to the people. I stepped into her shoes and felt her confidence and ability. Soon I was able to speak as she did, mimicking her gestures and intonation. Once that was comfortable, I stood before the crowd and spoke as myself.

The process took a few weeks for me to feel secure. The following times I visualized, I added people to the audience usually about ten at a time until I was relaxed and happy talking to them. I added more until they numbered 120 people in the crowd. During the time I was visualizing this, I was also writing my workshop, and starting to feel comfortable with the information I was planning to present. The big day came. I was very confident and felt totally at ease during my presentation, even when the power shut off and I lost my power point for about ten minutes. I carried on, not even blinking an eye as the tech person fidgeted around me, trying to get the power back on and the computer running. After my presentation, many people came to me and said how natural I was at speaking and that they learned a lot from my well organized seminar. I was thrilled and relieved and very happy that I had been able to put it all together. I learned to never underestimate the power of visualization and the help and nudges of my angels.

CHAPTER 3

COMMUNICATING WITH ANGELS

Up until this time in my life, I had received angel messages only when the angels decided to talk to me, or when communication was necessary for my well-being and safety. I decided that I wanted to initiate two-way conversations with the angels, in addition to the communication we had already established. I decided to try meditating, as I had heard many positive remarks about it, and had read some books regarding the process. A new friend of mine told me of an upcoming spiritual retreat weekend and told me: "When the student is ready the teacher will appear." I found that notion quite profound, so I signed up right away. The course turned out to be highly helpful; educating me about meditation. I was taught a great method of getting into meditation quickly. I was able to practice it many times that weekend, making it easy for me to continue at home. It was a method in which I focused on each colour of the rainbow, while relaxing each corresponding chakra. Each colour had a verse that went with it, designed to bring focus and more depth with each additional breath. We must have done this meditation 20 times during the workshop, sometimes adding further meditation or visualization to the process.

After the workshop I meditated every day whenever I had some time. It may have been as little as two minutes or as much as 45 minutes. I knew that I had to consistently develop that part of my consciousness if I were to improve and go deeper in my meditations. I thought augmenting my meditative skills was the only way for me to connect with the angels at will. I learned to pluck out distracting thoughts calmly and discard them. This was accomplished by visualizing the unwanted thought as a dark cloud, and gently grabbing it with my hand and tossing it away. I was taught to condition my mind so that unimportant noises would bring me into a deeper meditation. For instance, when I heard a noise, I said to myself, "When I hear noises, I now go deeper and deeper into meditation," as I dismissed the sound.

I got to the point where I had such deep meditations that I could no longer feel my body surrounding me. It felt as if my soul, the true me, was being lifted out of my body. I could see and feel my soul rise above my head and remain there, silent and serene, completely full of light and securely connected to Spirit. I was encouraged to experience this so I would understand that the soul is its own entity. The body is meant to house the soul for the purpose of life on Earth. The body is like the house you live in and the soul is the true being residing within. Each soul has an individual spiritual purpose. The soul is full of light from Source/Spirit/Higher Power. I was truly full of bliss during these meditations and felt the unity of the Universe and Oneness with my Creator and All There Is.

This was a very amazing discovery for me and one that changed the way I lived and thought. I no longer was interested in gaining material objects as I once had been. Instead I began to understand my true spiritual reasons for coming to the Earth plane. I started to look more deeply into life and all it had to offer. I went on nature walks in forests and parks, sitting against trees, absorbing their energy and feeling the earth in my hands. I was given lots of opportunity to see and get close to wildlife. I felt the calm and focused energy of animals; I observed coyotes, squirrels, birds, foxes, a bald eagle, a cougar, deer, rabbits, porcupines, herons, geese, and ducks and so on. I felt at home and peaceful near water, hence I frequented beaches, sun and surf as much as possible. I walked my dog for increasingly longer hikes in as many natural parks as I could find feeling creation all around me, breathing it into the inner most part of my being. The energy of Mother Earth became very compelling and intriguing as it penetrated me with its effervescent energy. It became very clear to me that I was a spirit having a human experience and not the other way around. This realization of experience in itself had a profound change within me and spurred me onto learning more, asking more questions and reading as many books as I could find about spirituality.

I decided to try to communicate with my guardian angel or any angel who would be interested in communicating with me. I wanted to receive guidance for my life and the direction I was to take in order to follow my Light Path and stay there. I asked my guardian angel to give me a physical indication that I could recognize as a "yes" answer. I asked simple questions at first such as, "Is my name Jill?" I tried this for a few days and finally got a really wonderful warm feeling in my heart. I adopted this as my guardian angel answering me with an affirmative to my question. I was so thrilled, that I then asked for a physical indication for a "no" answer. This proved to be a more difficult task as there was no indication forthcoming.

I began to formulate my questions so that I would get a "yes" answer. If I asked a question and felt nothing, I would turn the question around so that I would get a "yes" answer. For instance, I would ask "Is it a good idea to take this upcoming workshop?" If I felt nothing, then I would ask "Is it a better idea to *not* take the upcoming workshop?" If I received a yes answer, I would confirm the answer by rewording the question "Is it best to stay away from the workshop?" Again I would receive a "yes" answer confirming the first answer.

This worked fairly well as long as I remained in an unemotional state. As soon as I put any emotion, positive or negative into the asking, I would not receive a true answer. If I was having trouble keeping my emotions calm, I would pretend I was a fly on the wall or an observer, watching me ask the question. This helped as my emotions were kept within the "me" on the wall. The emotions stayed clear of the "me" who asked the question.

I kept working on receiving a "no" answer. It was about three months later when I felt a tightening in my jaw and a sick or yucky feeling in my abdomen. I adopted this as the "no" answer from my guardian angel. After that I began formulating questions that would require either a "yes" or "no" answer. This made the question and answer period progress a lot faster as I now received the correct answer straight away and no longer needed to reframe the questions again and again.

I had been meditating for at least three months when I met a woman who did written readings through Automatic Writing. I decided to give it a try. She taught me the following. I was to write a question down on a piece of paper. With the same paper in front of me, pen in hand, sitting in writing position, I was to put myself into a deep state of meditation. I was to allow my hand to write at will while remaining in my meditative state with my eyes closed. At first, I got squiggles and such, but after a few times, I started to write words and phrases. I didn't know what I had written until I came out of the meditation and read it. Sometimes I would receive a logical response that was on topic and fairly knowledgeable and other times, I wrote seemingly meaningless unrelated words. I would sometimes just get feelings with no words. Other times I would write words in some different language that I couldn't decipher. I kept working with this concept and within a month or two I was writing in the English language fairly consistently and on topic. Occasionally the information was not on topic, but at least it was coming in faster and being translated into words that I could decipher and that had a good message. Soon after, I began to write really quickly, and still couldn't keep up with the information channelling through. I realized that automatic writing bypasses the doubting mind and travels directly through the nervous system to the hand. This method was enough to turn on the faucet for my intuitive energy to flow much more quickly.

I decided to try responding orally to my written questions. This worked quite well and I practiced this as often as I could, still writing the question on a piece of paper before entering meditation. I found that when I needed to use my mind to ask a question, it brought me out of the meditative state. Writing the questions ahead of time kept my mind quiet and allowed me to remain in a deep state. This whole process took many months and many hours of time, the latter of which was not very available to me. After a while I found that I could remain in a light to medium level of consciousness and still get the same results as when in a deeper meditation. Because of this new lighter level of meditation, I could now use my mind to ask questions and still remain in a deep enough state to hear the answers.

Finally, I decided it was time to try to do readings for my friends. I had a few volunteers, so the experimental readings began. I asked my friends to have questions prepared for the sessions. Generally the answers came fairly slowly and sporadically at first. Occasionally information would gush in, and

I would receive it so quickly in words, pictures and feelings. It came all at once; I couldn't relay it to my friend fast enough. I would miss a lot of what was said and was unable to recall what had been transferred to me. I was being bombarded with information overload. It was a challenge to answer the question and address its multiple aspects. Sometimes I could feel the etheric energy swirling around me while an answer was being formulated, and it would take several minutes before I could grasp its meaning. Other times it was like pouring molasses on a cold winter day: the information flowed very s-l-o-w-l-y one word at a time.

The inconsistency of the information stream was due to my lack of focus, clarity, calmness and my inability to remain in the present moment. I recognized that it was vital for me to overcome these flaws in order to receive the delicate messages and convey them precisely to my client. In the beginning I would get excited when the etheric energy started channelling through me, and this would block or slow down the flow. I had to learn to be very calm and relaxed throughout the sessions in order for the energy to flow evenly and consistently.

After a while I began getting messages from unwanted, negative sources. I called my mentor, Krystal and she said: "Once you are open, you are open to everything." I decided to never communicate with any dark energy, so she advised me how to protect myself against it. This alone was quite a lengthy process before I was able to eliminate the darkness altogether. Every time I began my meditation for the purpose of communicating with angels, I was to say a prayer that she had given me, asking for safety and say that I would only receive information from a source of light. I was to protect myself from the darkness by a method I will describe in detail later in the book. It was very important for me to have no fear whatsoever of the dark side. My mentor told me that you can only get hurt from that which you believe in. Until my connection with the light side was firmly established, the darkness slipped in every so often, but only when I regressed and allowed the fear in. Like attracts like, so I had to be very persistent in my focus on the Light at all times. Gradually, these incidents surfaced less often and once I completely lived in faith that the angels would keep me safe, I did not receive dark messages any more. I cannot emphasize enough how important thoughts are!

I did have one incident when I felt a very sinister and daunting presence engulf me. I was visiting with two women whose acquaintance I had just met. I could see a dark shadow around one of them so I immediately protected myself from her energy. The visit continued far past my tolerance and I became quite tired. One of the women recounted a scary story about a haunted house that she had visited. At first I was resilient feeling protected. At some point in the story I felt myself falling to a place of fear only for a few seconds, but that was enough for a dark entity that she carried to enter me. Presently I stood up putting an end to the visit. The women left and immediately I knew something was terribly wrong with me.

My mind felt like it was rapidly deteriorating. I have never felt so out of control and unlike myself. It was very terrifying. I called in the most powerful angels I knew at the time to help me. They showed me in my mind's eye the Tree of Grounding. It was located a half hour drive away followed by a half hour walk. I rushed to the tree as quickly as my legs would carry me. I was guided as to what to say and do once I arrived at the base of the tree. I banished the dark entity from me and allowed the roots of the tree to hurl it down deep into

Mother Earth where she dissolved it completely and safely in her molten lava.

Instantly I returned back to my normal self, what a huge relief! My guardian angel told me that I underwent this episode to help me understand and empathize with people who carry dark entities; it was to make me stronger. I was advised that part of the duality on Earth is light and dark, that darkness does exist and it tries to stop the light from expanding. It can enter only if a person is afraid of, or believes in it. Without delay I resolved to always be more powerful in my light and to never allow darkness a foothold again. I emerged from this ordeal much stronger and with the complete faith that the light side is *always* more powerful than the dark. I now know that when one lives completely in the Light, darkness does not exist for them.

I remember wondering at the beginning of my journey if all of this spiritual stuff was real or just imagined. I had a lot of doubts about ethereal energy and was quite conflicted about spirituality. I wondered how or if it related to religion, and the concept of God that I had become apprehensive about in church so many years before. Did coincidences actually exist? Was all the information I received being purposely placed right in my hands through some guiding force? I developed an awareness that I needed to recognize spiritual messages as such. Being grateful with a sense of knowing that they were divinely planned, I thought this might attract more divine messages to me. I asked a question one day during a meditation, hoping to get an answer immediately. I asked for information that would help me solve a very troubling series of events that had been happening in my family. No intelligence emerged, so finally feeling dejected I gave up.

The next morning, I heard a knock at the door. I opened

the door to a woman who was giving away religious magazines. I was about to say no thanks, but instead gasped, as I
saw the cover of the magazine. To my utter surprise, the main
article was the answer to the very same question I had asked
the day before in my meditation! I grabbed the magazine
enthusiastically. Hurriedly I shut the door, thanking the startled woman under my excited breath. Immediately I read a
very helpful article that aided me in my quest for understanding precisely my specific topic. Not yet knowing about the Law
of Attraction, I never-the-less understood that something big
and amazing had happened and it spurred me on.

I decided on the spot that there is no such thing as coincidence. Everything that is asked for earnestly is answered
one way or another. Information came to me at first in written
articles or people speaking to me. Gradually this developed
into the angels giving me opportunities to increase my spirituality by leading me to particular places or events. Soon I was
able to communicate with the angels throughout my day, without the need to be in meditation. While I was performing my
everyday work and hobbies, the angels would give me ideas,
and ask me to do things and tell me interesting information.

I learned through trial and error that there are different
levels of angels. Higher levels of angels gave the most helpful
information. Sometimes I got messages from what I assumed
to be angels, who randomly gave me notions that were silly at
best and precarious at worst. Other times I would be provided
with concepts that were helpful and grounded. I became very
confused, and felt uneasy and unsafe and eventually chose to
stop following the angel's advice. One day, I became so frustrated after following what developed into potentially harmful
instruction, that I decided I would not talk to the angels any
more. About a day later, I got a message: "Why don't you ask

about the level of angels and with whom you are speaking."
When I got home, I went into a deep meditation and asked.

I found out that the angels who had given me suspect
guidance were really not angels at all. Some of the voices I'd
heard could be loosely considered as "angels-in-training".
They were very excited about learning, and wanted to help,
but did not have much experience about Earth life. I would
hear them talking to each other about silly ideas and esca-
pades. Because my hearing was so acute, I could hear them
whereas normally they would have no communication with
a person. Other voices I heard that were asking me to do
dangerous things were etheric energies posing as angels but
were akin to mischievous children and were not to be trusted
either. During my meditation I was counselled as to what level
of angels would be safe for me to speak with. I was advised
that considering my present proficiency, the highest level that
I could consistently communicate with was what they referred
to as the 7th level of angels.

From that minute forward, I decided I would speak
only to the 7th level angels and above. Once this new rule was
initiated, I no longer received misinformation, or any communication from angels other than the specified ones. This
renewed my confidence in the angels, and I became peaceful
and relaxed again, knowing I could trust their counsel. Eventually I was able to speak to increasingly higher levels of angels,
as I became clearer, more trusting and more grounded in my
skills. A few months later, I was sanctioned to talk to the 8th
level, and a month after that, the 9th level. This pattern carried
on to the 12th level. This escalation in levels for communication continued, and continues still.

It became apparent to me that I needed to be clearing
myself continually. I found that when I felt out of sorts or

generally stressed or unhappy, I could not hear the angels clearly. The angels taught me how to do clearing visualizations to improve my clarity, peacefulness and happiness which in turn enabled me to hear them much more powerfully. The first clearing they taught me was the "white light tornado clearing" and there were many more that followed.

Clients asked me how I stayed motivated and inspired to do spiritual work. Several events come to mind that really stimulated me to continue with my spiritual journey. When my boys were quite young, I drove to the school to pick them up for a dental appointment. They were not in the usual pick-up place, and I waited for a while. I wondered if they had forgotten about the appointment, and thought that they had probably walked home. I drove back home to find they had not arrived there either. By this time, it was quite late and I was concerned. This was an unusual happening so I phoned the school to see if anyone knew where they were. The principal answered and said she did not know where they were, but she would ask their teachers and call me back.

I decided to centre myself and go into a meditation. I asked: "Where are my boys?" Immediately I received a visual pretty much in the form of a video. It showed me them working in the school library, then leaving it and walking along one of the three roads that led to our home. I recognized the road as the video was playing, so got into the car and drove to the street that was shown. Sure enough, they were just a little farther along the road from where I had seen them in my visualization. When we returned home I discovered that the principal had left me a voice message saying that my boys had been in the library, but were now walking home. The confirmation that my intuitive video had been correct was a triumphant turning point; boosting my confidence that I was receiving correct information. This confirmed to me how much of a benefit it was for me to keep increasing my intuition. From that time forward, if I was concerned about the safety of my boys, I was able to get at least a message of a warm and safe feeling, and words corroborating this to me. This trustworthy communication became extremely helpful to me as they progressed through their teenage years during all the shenanigans that naturally ensued.

Another time I recall was when my oldest son had signed up for a film course in Hollywood. I thought he was much too young and inexperienced to travel by himself for the first time, across the continent, to a destination which he had only read about and knew no one. He left a voicemail from the Calgary Airport saying he had missed his connecting flight, and met a fellow traveller with whom he was leaving the airport for a while. He was scheduled on the next available plane which would take off five hours from then. Of course this was a huge concern for me. Who was this guy? Was my son safe? Would he return in time for his flight? There had been several abductions from airports recently and I became filled with fear.

When Tyler was scheduled to fly, we called the airport to get information. Because of the privacy laws, we were unable to ascertain whether Tyler had boarded the plane or not. We left a message on his phone, asking him to call us as soon as possible. We had five hours to wait till the plane landed. Either he would return the call, or we would be summoning the Calgary police to file a missing persons report.

Once there was nothing more to be done, I finally was able to retreat to a silent place where I contacted Tyler's angels. They showed me a visual of him on the plane, and told me that he was safe. Even though I trusted the angels it was a huge relief when Tyler called from Los Angeles safe and sound. Tyler's angels also said they would keep him safe while he was there. This made me feel much better, especially when he told me he was living in a really bad part of town, riding his longboard down the street at midnight while listening to his iPod. No amount of advising or warning from me could change his mind about how or when to travel the roads. Needless to say I was very relieved and thanked his angels profusely when he returned home safely!

I was constantly being drawn to spiritual things. I would often be encouraged to enter a book store and walk down a certain isle and look up just at the right time to find a book that caught my eye. Invariably it turned out to be perfect for my next phase of learning, as information I gained from this book was just what I needed at the time to understand a happening in my life. Sometimes a book stirred me and boosted me forward on my path. I would be guided into random stores that had an item I was to purchase that helped in my journey, such as stone stores, where I was drawn to certain crystals or energy stones that emanated beneficial energy to me. I was often led to turn on a specific radio station while driving. Sure enough there would be a song playing that contained some specific spiritual information to aid me, or a talk show that was on topic of what was troubling me in my life. I would be directed to play a certain CD and then guided to keep stopping it as I was told how each line referred to instances in my life. Newspaper and magazine articles of a helpful nature were practically dumped on my lap. License plates and street signs often held a piece of information I was looking for. People I met in the supermarket or at a gathering would broach a subject that I had been inquiring about. They consistently had a good solution for my problem unbeknownst to them. I was being showered with spiritual information that answered questions I had been asking. I decided to ask for angel help in becoming the angel reader that I had been working towards since my visit with Krystal.

Very soon after, a friend introduced me to a wonderful woman named Ann Lay, who drew and painted angels. We connected immediately and deeply as like-minded companions. I provided an angel reading for her and she gave me some of her beautifully painted angel greeting cards. She was impressed enough that she asked me to do readings for her friends. Ann advised me that I should accept fair exchange for the readings. I was inadequately employed at the time and Christmas was approaching, so I eagerly accepted her kind and generous offer. The following week she arranged two mornings for me to channel angel readings for eight of her friends. Fortunately Ann's friends were also impressed and they proceeded to tell their friends and so on. The number of my readings grew by word of mouth from this simple beginning. I am and will forever be grateful to Ann for her friendship and for instigating my spiritual work as an angel reader.

At this time one of the items I asked for on my manifestation list was enlightenment. The angels took this request very seriously as they began several years' worth of educational events that are still occurring. For instance, they revealed a topic to me that I was to scrutinize, and then directed to a specific incident that would evoke my negative emotions such as witnessing a confrontation of sorts or a sad or upsetting experience. They asked me questions such as "Why do you think we showed you this?" or "What can you learn from this situation?" Similarly, when the angels took me to a location for the purpose of educating me, they asked me "Why do you think we brought you here?" or "What is it that you can learn from this site?" Always there was a lesson to learn; most often to release judgment, or negativity of some sort, or to expand my horizons so I could keep progressing on my soul path.

They continually encouraged me to develop my own aptitude to analyse life, and learn every possible concept from each event I experienced and how it related to me. At the beginning I was grateful for just one idea though soon I was urged to ask them, "How many more things are there that I can learn?" Inevitably there were three or more additional notions for me to examine.

I began to ask the angels these same questions to understand why I felt out of sorts on any particular time or day. I learned that it was important to ask for help correctly. Following the precept "God or Spirit helps those who help themselves," I was guided to ask in the following manner. "Please *help me* to discover the reasons why I am feeling upset today." Conversely if I asked them to "Tell me what's wrong", or to" Fix this problem," I would not get a response. Asking correctly is the key to receiving the correct answer. Angel education was at first primarily designed for me to recognize within myself negative aspects that required clearing. This improved my ability to receive intuition, eventually enabling me to tap into all appropriate information and wisdom in the Universe.

My main desire was to be happy. I stated this many times to my angels and they guided me to learn countless things that helped me with this goal. There were many times in my early years that I would have been much relieved and more contented had I only known how to listen to my intuition better. Once I learned this skill, my life became much more understandable and therefore palatable. I found that fear evolves from a lack of understanding. Once I understood a given situation, my fear dissipated, allowing me the peace to move forward.

Even though the challenges in my life did not get easier, in fact they became much more difficult; I had access to an inner knowing that eventually everything would work out for the best. I was able to see life from other people's perspectives, which aided in my growing ability to be empathetic to other's reactions and ideas. I foresaw that undesirable events were necessary for spiritual growth of my loved ones and me. I can only say that this was an innate knowledge and wisdom that gradually surfaced as I became more in tune with the subtle energies floating in the ethers. Many times horrendous incidents happened, that during the initial stages appeared there could be no positive outcome. However time passing proved that there was goodness and light in all the seemingly negative events that occurred. I achieved a lot of learning that I could not have acquired any other way. Mentally and emotionally processing my reactions from these events propelled me forward on my path. Eventually my intuitive ability brought peace into my life and it is for this reason that I encourage others to accept and increase their own intuitive abilities.

CHAPTER 4

ANIMAL COMMUNICATION

Many years before I discovered spirituality and intuition, and before I had any inkling that I could communicate with animals, my horse Toby sent me a very strong message. It was early in his colic episode that was explained previously. I had been following the veterinarian's advice to keep walking him so he would not roll. She said that if he rolled on the ground there was a large possibility that his condition could worsen; that his gut might twist inflicting him with more pain. We had been walking for hours, but there were a few times that day in between his bouts of pain when he became calm and relaxed. During one of those much needed interludes from his wearisome condition, I lead him to his stall to rest. He stood quietly beside me, nuzzling me peacefully and gratefully.

Presently I received a picture in my head of Toby lying dead on the floor. The clarity of the vision startled me and penetrated me to my core. I quickly shook that image out of my thought process, rejecting it completely. I continued to care for him as best I could. I was not ready yet to accept his death. A few years later I realized that Toby was giving me a message; he was dying, his time was up. Had I listened to his telepathic communication, I could have saved him a lot of discomfort from the vet checks and the trailer ride to Guelph, and all the pointless agony that ensued. I understood that had I been able to communicate with him, I could have handled the situation better and could have helped him much more in his time of need. I have since learned that pets and people will often project a message to their care-giver that their life is almost finished. People are often not willing to receive this communication at the time, but may reflect on it later. Pets will sometimes prolong their lives so as to allow their loved ones time to prepare for their upcoming loss.

My subsequent notion of interspecies communication happened during a Horse Trial while I was riding a friend's horse. This horse was without a doubt the strongest bossiest horse I had ever ridden. She and I were on our first cross country course together and only the third time I had ridden in a Horse Trial Competition.

A Horse Trial is when horse and rider partake in three disciplines: dressage, cross country, and stadium jumping, all to be completed in one day. Dressage is when horse and rider perform a test consisting of a sequence of movements in walk, trot and canter. The performance is judged for the most part on balance, suppleness, obedience and harmony. Cross Country is ridden at a fast canter or gallop. Horse and rider must cross rivers, and jump banks, ditches, combinations, obstacles, into or out of water, and on uphill and downhill grades. Stadium jumping is just what it infers; jumping obstacles in a stadium.

The rider walks through the jumping courses ahead of time, but the horse is not allowed to see the jumps. Once in the starting box, my horse became very excited and I did my best to calm her. As we began the cross country course I sharpened my focus on galloping over the obstacles.

Presently I slid into a deep state of awareness; deeper than I ever before experienced. It felt as if time did not exist anymore. In retrospect it felt as if I was in an active type of meditation, intently cognizant of my surroundings, and extremely focused on accomplishing this new endeavour.

Suddenly my senses were extraordinary. I could see far into the distance so clearly, I could hear every minute detail; the birds singing, the wind rustling in the leaves and the cars far away on the road. I felt every footstep and heartbeat of the horse as she sprinted along the course. After we traversed the first obstacle there was a long gallop before the next jump. I looked to the left and my horse looked to the left. I looked to the right and my horse looked to the right. I felt as if we were one being. I have never felt so connected to another individual. It was as if I could read her mind and she could read mine. We continued onto the next fence and I felt myself warning her of the rocks lying in front of the jump so she would not spook. I knew deep within me that she understood. Before the next jump I explained to her about the flags blowing in the wind; and by the following jump about the brightly coloured plastic flowers. She seemed to really understand me. I was sending pictures from my mind to hers. This communication appeared to be developing from my deeply conscious state of awareness. I was preparing myself for the next jump, from my recollection of walking through the course. All the while she was listening and processing the information too.

Later in the season we were on another cross country course and I told her ahead of time that there was a particularly quick turn very soon after one of the jumps. This mare habitually accelerated after each jump into a very fast gallop that would prevent us from making the turn.

She seemed to understand my direction, and as we got close to the jump I reminded her again. As we approached the jump I could feel her body collecting into a short stride. She took the jump, landed and remained in a short stride. To my delight, I could see her looking for the opening in the fence line that I had previously advised her of! We completed the turn smoothly and swiftly as if it was second nature to her. The owner of the horse was standing close by and obviously was very aware of the mare's normal behaviour. She was quite surprised that we had made the turn, and so smoothly, and acknowledged that to me later.

Armed with this exhilarating experience, I started wondering if I could communicate with animals in other situations. My angels, always eager to help, advised me to re-enact my mental focus that I had discovered during the cross-country course. I decided to examine the state I had been in. I explored the procedure I had taken, by breaking it down into individual steps that I could identify and replicate at will. I wanted to teach this amazing skill to other people. I treated it as a mystical equation. Being in the present moment +extreme focus + heightened awareness = telepathic communication or "horse-telepathy."

My interest in animal communication increased further because of my innate desire for safety. Whenever I couldn't master my fear, or my horse skills were inadequate, I felt strongly that horse telepathy may be my only way of ensuring or at least hoping to ensure my safety. On several occasions I was told by riding instructors that I had a natural seat and that I could ride much better than my limited riding experience would normally allow. In the beginning, I was directed to my mounts by my riding instructors, but in later years, I would be offered horses to ride, and I would seemingly know from my intuition, when I checked it, which ones were safe and which ones were not.

I didn't always think to engage help from my inner voice, and one such time was when I was training Thoroughbred horses. These horses had been recently retired from the racing industry, and it was my job to train them to begin new lives as mounts for challenged or disabled riders. Anyone who knows horses would probably find this ludicrous as race horses are often far too energetic and spooky to be safe for a beginner or a compromised rider. A small chestnut mare who was difficult at best gave me the ride of my life! I had been riding her for a couple of weeks with limited success. One day the owner's son grabbed the reins while I was mounted and the horse reacted severely. She bucked like she was in a bucking bronco contest, dumping me face first on the dirt and rocks, causing me a huge black eye, bruised face, sprung rib, and lots of pain. That was the last time I did not check in with my intuition about whether it was safe to ride a given horse.

Shortly after this incident an acquaintance of mine John, kindly offered me his very well trained retired Event horse to ride. Eclipse was an Anglo-Arab and was talented, very smart and highly energetic almost to a fault. He knew his job, and was determined to do everything his way. He galloped at the fences with break-neck speed, and all I could do was hang on and hope that we would both survive. Despite this, I decided to take him to a Horse Trial. After many days of practicing with him for the show, he would still gallop through the stadium fences, knocking them down instead of jumping over them. I asked his owner what I was doing wrong and how I could improve. John replied that Eclipse had always had the habit of knocking down stadium fences. In many shows, even with John who was a much more experienced rider than I was, they had not accomplished many clear rounds. I decided to talk to Eclipse about this problem. I had heard several times that once people are open to communicating through the ethers, they are open to everything. I thought the horse-consciousness might just be a different frequency that I would need to locate and access. I asked the angels for help in communicating with him. Angels will help you do just about anything that is helpful for your progress and safety. The animals we share this planet with are very important to the angels, and they want all earth dwellers to live harmoniously together, including understanding each other.

A few days later, Eclipse and I had a conversation, guided by the angels; the first premeditated telepathic communication I had ever had with any animal. I led him to an isolated pasture so he would not be distracted by the other horses. I sat near him, just outside the paddock and went into a meditative state while he munched softly on the sweet spring grass. It was a quiet and calm day at the barn, so I knew I would be able to concentrate on my mission for however long it would take.

I had read a book previously that explained that the best way to communicate with animals was in pictures. It said that animals understand pictures not words and that is how they speak with each other. I decided to convert the words that I wanted to say to Eclipse into pictures. I focused on what to say in a simple and direct manner. I visualized a picture of me speaking to him. My intent was to ask his permission to communicate with him, as it is important to not invade privacy. He seemed very surprised and after a while I sensed he replied: "Yes, of course." I created a picture in my head of him jumping. I then sent him a picture of him knocking the poles down as he was jumping. I tried several times, but I was not getting any response. I thought for a minute, and decided to focus very hard and went deeper into meditation. In my mind I developed a video-visualization of him racing at the jumps and knocking them down along with the intended question of why he did that. I projected this to him, throwing all of my telepathic energy into this communication. A few minutes later he replied to me directly. To my surprise and delight, Eclipse played a video back to me of him galloping wildly, knocking down the jumps; his only concern was racing over the finish line, as fast as he could. He also sent me sensations of fervent desperation and fierce anxiety in completing his self-appointed assignment. His message included the sensation that he had done his best to do what the rider wanted.

Eclipse had no understanding whatsoever that his job was to also clear the jumps. I suddenly understood the miscommunication between humans and horses. No one ever explains to horses or other animals what we expect their role to be in our lives. They are left guessing as to what we want them to do. I sent another video to him. In the video, Eclipse was cantering at a slower pace, carefully clearing the jumps. I felt his astonishment substantially. I was filled with a considerably strong feeling that he understood my communication.

The next week, John gave Eclipse and I a jumping lesson. John was astounded that Eclipse was jumping so carefully and relaxed and leaving the fences intact. Eclipse was so proud and happy as he strutted around the riding arena. He seemed relieved that he didn't have to race like a maniac over the jumps. John couldn't fathom the change in his horse and even said, "Maybe Eclipse isn't feeling well today." I just smiled and said, "I think he's feeling better than he ever has." I was not confident enough at the time to give an explanation to John about my newly developing horse communication skills. I was very close-mouthed about my telepathic and intuitive abilities in the early days.

John had been to many dressage shows with Eclipse and was able to control his horse easily. Eclipse knew I was less experienced and he and would second guess and overrule my aids, frequently accelerating his gait changes in the dressage ring. I tried my best to contain his exuberance, but inevitably he would become excited. He would act out and change his gait before the designated letter marking the spot where the change was required. He was an enthusiastic over-achiever, always wanting to do more than the best job possible. I knew he did not understand the precision in which the test must be ridden. I thought if only he could comprehend the process of showing and the specifics of judging he would relax more. Maybe he would feel confident in me, and follow the direction I was giving him. I wanted Eclipse to understand what I expected of him.

I decided to teach him dressage as I would a person. In the following weeks, I taught him the letters which were the markers for the four corners and long walls of the dressage ring. I audibly said the name of the letter as I walked him past each one. Communication became much easier as we both attuned ourselves to each other's telepathic energy. I still spoke to him in pictures, but also began to speak to him in words. Once he knew the letters, I projected to him a video of him doing his gait transition while his body was in the middle of the letter (not 15 feet before the letter!) When practicing in the ring, I told him with telepathy what he was to do when we got to each letter, following the test that we would be performing at the show. I projected to him a running commentary for example, at "A" canter, at "C" walk, at "X" halt and so on. Soon he understood what I expected of him.

Eclipse having this knowledge was such a wonderful help for us both. From that day forward, he became very accurate at changing his gait precisely when he was positioned at the middle of the correct letter. He listened intently for the next telepathic directive from me. He became more relaxed and confident in his movements. He completely released his habit of prematurely anticipating his next gait change. Dressage became very enjoyable for us both. Eclipse didn't have to worry anymore; he knew what to do and when to do it. Just as with people, once a horse or any animal understands their situation or job, fear dissipates and peacefulness emerges.

I also wanted Eclipse to understand what his purpose was according to the judges who would be scrutinizing every movement at the competition. I projected to him a video of the judge marking the test, and the important things he needed to do that would gain points. I explained the whole Horse Trial show process to him. Finally I had the impression that he understood. Over the following few weeks, he learned to understand me when I spoke in words, so I didn't have to keep projecting videos. He was so amazing and never missed a directive. He was always waiting in delighted anticipation for me to speak to him. I was so proud of him. He was so smart! He's probably the most intelligent and most eager to learn horse I have ever known. Eclipse was so thrilled to be speaking with me; I'm not sure who was more excited about our new communication skills, him or me!

The following month I took Eclipse to our first Horse Trial together. We aced the accuracy portion of the dressage test. We were both so focused on the telepathic communication that I neglected to encourage the cadence and forward motion necessary to win the class. That had not been my intention. I was extremely thrilled that Eclipse had listened to my instructions so clearly, especially considering all the noise and distractions at the show. The stadium jumping went extremely well, with Eclipse clearing all the fences except the second to last. After he blasted through it sending the poles flying, he immediately apologized and said he got carried away with the moment! He then managed to collect himself and clear the last fence, passing by the timer in a relaxed and controlled canter.

Eclipse was a well-known horse in the area and many people approached me afterward, expressing their surprise at how well he cleared the jumps and how calm he was. John was the most surprised, and said it was rare for him to knock a fence down and then recover to clear the next, especially it being the last fence and so close to the finish line. He said that once Eclipse knocked down a fence, he would usually knock down most of the remaining jumps in the round.

I felt very blessed that I could communicate such a valuable lesson to Eclipse that would help him for the rest of his life. During the next phase of the show, the cross-country course, there was no wild galloping at any of the jumps! Eclipse was uncharacteristically laid-back; cantering peacefully, clearing the obstacles carefully and we both really enjoying the round feeling safe and secure.

Over the following few years I visited friends at other horse boarding facilities and boarded my horse, Jack, at several large stables. Every so often, I would ask a horse for permission to speak to him, hoping to expand my abilities of horse communication. Invariably they would be very surprised and reply with "Are you talking to me?" After a short conversation they would invariably ask me if I could teach their owners how to talk to them. Gradually random horses would somehow sense my ability and initiate a dialogue with me. I learned some interesting things, and enjoyed seeing their perspective on life. Often they were happy with their jobs and life which made speaking with them fun and rewarding. However, sometimes they told me how unhappy they were with their owner, their work, or with the facility where they were boarded. Often they would ask me to take them away to a better place, or ask me to become their owner. I knew I couldn't save all the horses, so I made suggestions to people of ways to make their horses more content. Unfortunately more often than not my voice fell upon unconcerned or sceptical ears. It became increasingly difficult for me to board at or visit larger busier barns, as I often empathically absorbed the discontent and upset, and left the facility with deep sadness for the horses.

I started looking for a small happy place to board my horse, and fortunately I quickly found a wonderful back yard boarding facility. I was so grateful and relieved to have escaped the projected messages from disgruntled horses. At the new place, all the horses were very happy, and it was and still is a pleasure boarding there. My friends who own the barn are very kind and good to the horses and me.

The first time I telecommunicated with my cat was the night before I took him to the veterinarian to have him put to sleep. During his life, Bobby was always a very happy cat who purred constantly throughout the day and night, and purred much louder when given attention. He always purred when the vet gave him his yearly exam and immunization injections. I remember one unfortunate night, when he was about a year old he got a clothes hanger caught in the back of his throat and I gently removed it as he thrashed around. Even as we were driving to the Afterhours Veterinary Clinic, with me sopping up his blood as it drained out of his mouth, he purred. As the veterinarian examined him and gave him his treatment, he purred.

Bobby was such a loving and kind cat. He had a personality similar to a dog. When we came home he would excitedly greet us at the door. When we went for walks he would follow us, darting behind bushes and hiding, then racing to the next bush taking cover again peeking through the leaves to see if we spied him. Sometimes he would simply walk beside us on the trail. Many people commented that he had human-like eyes.

As he aged his health slowly degenerated and when he was 19 years old, he stopped eating. I followed him around trying to interest him in eating various foods and concoctions I had created for him. He would eat a mouthful, and then wander off. By the third day of this, I went to pat him and he didn't purr. I called the vet immediately. She knew Bobby and said that if he was not purring, I better bring him in right away. Upon arrival at the animal clinic, the veterinarian examined Bobby and gave him some subcutaneous injections. She said this would either prompt him to eat again, or I was to bring him back the next day to be put to sleep.

Late that night after Bobby had not eaten anything all day, I put him on top of me as I lay on the couch. He remained perched there for a long time; he was uncharacteristically dull. I asked the angels to help me convey my message to him. I descended into a light meditation and asked him how he was feeling. He replied that he was very ill and dying. I asked him if he wanted to be put to sleep the next day, or if he wanted to live longer. I sent him a visual of the vet giving him an injection that would end his life. He replied that he would really appreciate me putting him to sleep in a quick and humane way. He added that if it was my need for him to remain alive, that he would be willing to do that for me. He was such a compassionate and giving cat. He added that he would live four more days, suffering with a lot of pain. I explained to him that I did not want him to suffer; I only wanted what was best for him. He then firmly asked me to put him to sleep.

The next afternoon at the appointed time, I took him to the vet. Bobby behaved so unlike his normal self. I'm sure this was partly because he was so ill, but he sat in my lap in the waiting room, not purring, not trying to escape. It seemed that he knew why he was there and he willingly and gratefully accepted his demise. Once in the vet's operatory, he lay on the table, consenting to the fatal injection, bravely and knowingly. I didn't have to hold him down as I usually did at his veterinary visits; I just patted him lovingly for the last time. Following the injection, his body lay on the table, lifeless.

Instantaneously I was astonished to see a bright light bounce up from within him and go to the corner of the room. I knew instinctively that this beautiful light was his soul. I felt such elation emanating from him; he was free! His soul was so happy and excited to be liberated from his cumbersome body. His soul-light, bounced around the room and repeatedly thanked me profusely. His emancipated light projected immensely happy energy. He stayed for probably no longer than a minute, made sure I was ok, and then whisked off elsewhere.

I had the feeling he was saying goodbye to the family; his soul advancing at lightning speed. I left the vet's office and began the trek home. Bobby's spirit zoomed back to me about fifteen minutes later as I was driving home. I felt his highly vibrational energy rush through me from head to toe. He had come to say his final goodbye. He was so ecstatic and appreciative, I just had to smile through my tears and feel happy for him. My son told me that day, as he walked home from school, that he felt Bobby's energy pass right through him. Bobby had been put to sleep minutes before my son felt this phenomenon. We have such wonderful memories of Bobby and all his hilarious antics.

Many years later our dog Heidi went missing just before a mandatory meeting with the new boss at my work. I asked my neighbour, who was also my dog sitter, to keep an eye out for Heidi as she had never disappeared before. Heidi did not return that day. I searched the whole area and especially around the house many times, and petitioned as many friends as I could to help look for her. I had a very dear friend and animal communicator Susan Wright, do a reading on her, and she said that Heidi had passed away. I knew this deep inside, but continued to search for her day in and day out just in case she was alive and needed help to come home. Ultimately I received a message that she did not want to be found as she didn't want me to be shocked by her appearance. She wanted me to remember her the way she looked when she was alive and attractive. When the time was right, she would allow me to find her.

Almost a week later, I had slowed my search enough to lie down in the sun for a few minutes around the pond that Heidi loved so much. As I finally relaxed for the first time in a week, a celestial voice asked me if I wanted to find Heidi now. I followed the Light energy into the forest, weaving around the trees. I was treading over the fallen logs when I came to an opening. Something caught my eye, but I kept walking. The voice said, "Stop, turn around." I did and looked down, right at Heidi's half-hidden decomposed body. I didn't recognize it as such, and decided to continue walking. The voice said louder to "come back and look again." I reluctantly looked again and this time saw Heidi's collar on her skeleton. I finally had closure. She had passed away in her favourite spot to wander and sniff. Strangely, that area had been searched the most, but her body had remained undetected. Heidi was such a wonderful and loving dog. She will remain right beside Bobby in our hearts forever.

I was guided one mid-summer evening to view the sunset, and was shown by an extrasensory photo where to go to have a great vantage point. I decided to take Jack, my horse, bareback to the specified grass field which was about two kilometres from his barn. My plan was to let him loose so he could eat grass and I could sit on a round bale and watch the sunset. I had set him free not long before in two different locations and each time after a short while he ran back to the barn. I decided to try one last time to see if he would be good and stay with me. Before I released him, I communicated to him through telepathic words and pictures that I wanted him to stay very close to me, otherwise I would not attempt to give him free range again. When I felt that he understood, I released him and sat on the ground about thirty feet away from him and went into a light meditation. When I peeked to see where he was, I could see he was keeping a close watch on me. He gradually grazed in a direct path toward where I was sitting. As he neared me I could see the adorable look in his eyes. I had the inner knowing that he was trying to be the absolute best he could possibly be, by following my instructions. Presently he grazed with his head right beside me so I could pat his face. He ate the grass right beside my foot and soon was nudging it with his muzzle to munch on the grass underneath. He then nibbled at the grass adjacent to my underside, nudging my back with his head. He couldn't have been closer! I laughed and told him he was a good boy. Some horses have such a good sense of humour! I walked about forty feet away from him along the side of the field, closer to the round bale on which I had been guided to sit. Once more Jack ate in a straight line through the field to where I was sitting, and again tried to graze on the grass right underneath me. I patted him on his neck and face. This time got up and strolled about sixty feet away and sat on the top of a round bale. The sunset was magnificent and I enjoyed it immensely. Jack ate his way directly toward me again. Once he reached me, he nuzzled my foot as it dangled from my perch. He lifted his head so I could pat him yet again. He had never been so affectionate before. He was such a good boy and had followed my directions perfectly.

The previous summer we had gone to the same location many times, where he had sauntered off into the field fairly far, and I had to retrieve him several times. I know he understood my talk with him that night as his behaviour was so dissimilar to what he had displayed in the past. I'm happy that he had the will to follow my direction. Animals are similar to you and me in that someone can ask us to do something, and we have the choice of whether to comply or not.

Many times through the years I had wondered how well horses could see in the dark. Previously Jack had rested every night in a stall inside a barn. Now he was being boarded outdoors which meant he was outside day and night. I was concerned for his safety. One night my guides advised me to ride Jack at dusk. I said it was too late and that it would be dark soon, but they insisted so I reluctantly mounted for what I thought would be a very short ride. In the past I had always brought Jack back to the barn just before dusk. I mounted and we walked out to a field that was about twenty minutes away. We watched the serene beautiful sunset over the adjacent forest and I lost track of time. We headed for home just as darkness was setting in.

By the time we reached the forest it was very dark and I could no longer see the path. I was worried as I knew there were many tree roots and rocks and lumps and bumps along the path; I didn't want Jack to trip or fall on them. I was just about to turn him around and head back to the smooth footing of the field, when my angels said to me, "Do you want to see how horses see in the dark?" Suddenly intrigued, I answered "yes." Instantly I could see the forest pathway easily; it was completely lit up! It had become a large tunnel of golden light.

It looked like a golden halo all around us. It swept thirty feet in front and behind us, and twenty feet high above us, lighting up the trees. Unexpectedly I had gained night vision! I could see the leaves on the trees and the uneven path very clearly. I was astounded at how well horses could see in the dark. It made sense to me as they must have had a way of living and grazing through the night when they existed in the wild. After about two minutes my vision returned to normal, causing me to struggle with invisible branches brushing against my face in the darkness of the night. I knew from this experience that Jack would be able to see well enough to get us home safely. I have never worried about horses seeing in the night since then.

I decided to take Jack to a couple of shows. The first one was managed by the Ontario Standardbred Adoption Society. Standardbreds are bred as harness race horses. After their usefulness as race horses, often they would be slaughtered. Adoption societies formed to give these beautiful horses a useful post-racing career. I am so grateful to all the adoption centres that help innocent animals find wonderful homes, and loving people to connect with. All the horses that had been adopted by OSAS were invited to participate in the show, along with other Standardbreds and their owners. I had adopted Jack several years earlier, so I jumped at the chance to go when my friend offered to trailer us there.

During the warm up and in between classes when I had some down-time, I noticed the energy of the people and their horses. I could see and feel the commitment of these riders and horses to each other. I could see in my mind's eye the long hours of lessons and hard work these people went through to teach their mounts to be riding horses. I saw them bathing their horses and braiding their manes and tails for the show.

They were so proud of their horses, as was I. I found myself hoping and wishing that everyone and their mount had a wonderful day; that everyone could take a ribbon home. Throughout the jumping classes, I was experiencing all the jumping rounds as if I was a part of each rider. I gasped with concern if their horse stumbled or refused a fence. I joyfully clapped when each horse and rider completed their round safely and happily.

I realized profoundly that competition with a driven desire to win was not part of my spiritual journey. I could see that everyone was a winner and I wanted to compete somehow where everyone finished as a champion.

CHAPTER 5

HOUSE CLEARINGS

I was invited to a workshop by a new friend of mine who was the only spiritually aware person I knew at the time. It was the first spiritual workshop that I attended. It was facilitated by a woman from British Columbia, named Krystal who did not often travel to the Toronto area, so I decided to participate. During the workshop she taught us how to see auras, and to sensitize our receptors to feel the subtle energies of rocks, trees and Mother Earth. We learned how to clear Geophysic Lines and Hartman Lines, which are invisible lines that anchor negative energy. These lines are detectable through dowsing, a process which is accomplished by using metal coat hangers, one in each hand, while walking slowly in a straight line until the hangers cross each other. We must have looked pretty funny, the five of us walking around the front lawn with coat hangers in our hands exclaiming our excitement when the coat hangers moved by themselves to our utter amazement. We also learned how to dowse for vortexes of energies. These are often formed above underground water currents. Vortexes are formed from positive or traumatic events which occurred in the past and the corresponding energy was absorbed into the earth.

This workshop was a turning point for me. Until this time, I wondered a lot about invisible forces and if they were just my imagination. Sure, I knew that radiation was an invisible beam of energy, but real and detectable on x-rays none the less. This and the dowsing really brought home to me that just because you can't see it, doesn't mean that it doesn't exist.

Krystal explained that these lines are what entities and spirits attach themselves to, and after the lines are eliminated, the spirits can be given the opportunity to see the light tunnel to the other side or Nirvana. This sounded very outrageous, so I decided to try it at home, more actually to prove that it was a bizarre idea than for anything else. A few days after the workshop, I had a couple of hours to myself. I initiated the sequence of elements necessary for clearing the lines including asking my angels for protection and help. The clearing seemed to take us a long time, but finally I felt it had been completed. I finished my day and went to sleep. There are specialty angels for all aspects of Earth life and clearing lost souls is of particular interest to the angelic realm. They want to help everyone who is in need, and ghosts are no exception. As more ghost-spirits with their negative energy are cleared, and replaced with peace and light, Earth's vibration becomes higher. Raising the vibration of Earth is one of the angels' priorities.

At 2 a.m., I was awakened alarmingly by the silhouette of a woman in a white dress standing beside my bed. It was a dress that would have been worn in the early part of the 1800's. She angrily told me that she was upset with me for weakening her foothold. I was bewildered but managed to utter: "How can I help you?" She didn't answer in words, but I had the feeling that she needed me to project a feeling of love to her. I sent as much love as I could muster, and fairly soon I saw her energy field light up. I could see the light tunnel opening up behind her. I directed her to turn around and go into the light. She did and I could see she began to smile. On her way into the light she said to me: "I'm sorry I frightened your son," and at the same time showed me how she had looked when she scared him. She had changed from her present state into an evil looking monster wearing a black shroud. Her sudden dark appearance reminded me of what my oldest son had described to me many times as the monster-dark reaper in his closet. She quickly returned to her original ghost state and swiftly jettisoned up the tunnel. A few seconds later, I had such a warm feeling come over me and I heard voices uttering "thank you." I felt such a huge sense of gratitude coming from the other side. This gratefulness emanated from her family of spirits who had been waiting patiently for her to cross over. They were ecstatic that she had finally joined them. I descended into a peaceful slumber.

In the early morning, I was awakened by the ghost silhouette of a man sporting a cowboy hat, cowboy boots and western clothing. He was dressed as if he was from the first part of the 1900's. He spoke with a lazy drawl and asked me what was to become of him. I sensed that he needed kindness so I projected that to this ghost-spirit and soon the light tunnel appeared behind him. He turned around and elevated up the tunnel. Again, his patiently waiting family of spirits thanked me and gave me a feeling of such deep gratitude. I remembered a time several years before when my son told me that a man in a cowboy hat had gotten into the car and had sat in the front seat while I was driving him to my parent's house. At the time I didn't quite know what to make of his observation, but finally after seeing this ghost, I understood.

About a day later, I saw the figure of a young boy about six years old, dressed in shorts with suspenders and a short-sleeved buttoned and collared shirt. He looked as if he would have been from the mid-1800's. He looked very frightened and I sensed he needed courage. I sent him courage and he started to smile. He said he had fun playing with my youngest son. He projected a picture to me of them playing together when my son was three years old. I immediately remembered a summer when my son had an imaginary friend who played with him often. Unfortunately, an adult relative told my son that it was silly to have an imaginary friend. He then became unable to see this wonderful playmate who had brought him so much fun, activity and laughter. The young boy ghost saw the light and went toward it, flowing into it as had the other ghost-spirits. When he got to the other side, his parents came to me and were crying with joy at having their son with them again. Their gratitude was so strong that I had tears of joy welling up in my eyes. I felt that it had been very important to help these earth-bound spirits and their families who were now able to continue their journeys, with their family intact.

A particularly interesting clearing was at a friend's house when I was invited there for dinner. The man of the house had mentioned to me that he felt his energy was always being drained from him, and that he had not felt well since he moved into this house about three years prior. I went upstairs to the washroom for a few minutes before dinner was served and on entering the room I heard a ghastly deep voice say with threatening force: "You don't belong here!" I knew immediately from previous clearings that this was a ghost who was revealing himself to me to scare me off. I looked at him and said: "Actually it's you who doesn't belong here." Instantly, I began the clearing work. I knew that if there was any delay, the ghost could go into hiding rendering it difficult and time-consuming to locate him again. I protected myself against his negative energy and called in my "clearing angels." We projected a sensation of love to him. He resisted for what seemed like a long time but gradually accepted the offering. I have found so far that no matter how dark an entity is, they cannot resist light energy for more than a few minutes because love is always much more powerful than fear. After several minutes, he smiled and said he had never felt love in his life. He thanked me profusely and admitted that he had been extracting the energy from the man in the house and that he was sorry. The light tunnel appeared behind him and I encouraged him to turn and step into it. Before he left, he said that he had been a sea captain. He ran away from home when he was 14 years old, choosing a life at sea, desperately fleeing from his abusive father. He showed me a glimpse of his life as a youngster and it was very frightful indeed. I asked the angels to bless him and to help him find his way. I saw two angels descend from the tunnel, and with one on each side of the sea captain, the three of them ascended up the tunnel. I was given a very warm and wonderful feeling once the captain had reached the other side. I returned to the kitchen just in time for dinner, and after a wonderful meal and a great visit I went home.

The next morning upon awakening I saw in my mind's eye two white light beings looking in the kitchen window of my same friend's home. They appeared to be a married couple, in their light tunnel, very much on a mission with their hands waving above their heads. I could see they were very focused on an intense pursuit. I kept saying to them, "Go up the tunnel," but they steadfastly refused. Since this was one of the first clearings I did, I wasn't sure what was happening. I phoned my friend and asked if there was anything odd happening at the kitchen window. He said that the cat kept jumping up on the counter and staring out the window. This was a new and strange behaviour for the cat, and my friend was perplexed as to why it was acting in this odd way. I told him what I had seen and then I went to work on it straight away. I tried to talk to the couple outside the window, but was unable to in their panic-stricken state. They were much harried, with their hands waving in the air above their heads similar to someone treading water to keep afloat. I realized they were treading the light energy to keep themselves on Earth. I called in my angel helpers to look around the house to see if any more ghosts were hiding out. Sure enough, in the far corner of the basement was a young boy about eight years old wearing a vintage school uniform. I asked him to come out, but he was too afraid. He said there was a nasty man-ghost that he was hiding from. I told him that the man ghost had been cleared away and that it was safe for him to emerge. I suspected that the couple in the light was his parents, not willing to leave their post without him. The boy finally emerged from his seclusion and I guided him to the window, reuniting the family. They were all crying with happiness. They quickly went up the light tunnel, and then filled me with such heartfelt appreciation that I joined them in their tears of joy. The light tunnel disappeared after they ascended. I called my friend to tell him of the proceedings, and asked him to let me know what was happening with respect to his cat's behaviour. That afternoon he called to say that the cat was no longer preoccupied with the kitchen window and had indeed returned to his normal activity. Animals and cats in particular are able to see or at least sense paranormal activity.

Another outstanding clearing involved a very old home, built in the early 1800's. It had a lot of negative energy. The owner of the house had on many occasions felt and seen ghosts in the house, but did not specify her concerns to me. Her son-in-law had also seen some unwanted ghost characters around the house and grounds and was uncomfortable visiting there. I was guided by my angels to take a helper with me as there were many spirits to release, so I asked my son, Tyler to go with me. We arrived at the house and immediately felt the negative vibes. We asked our guardian angels to protect us from the dark energy and called in the clearing angels. The house owner ushered us into the living room where I felt a male presence. Tyler immediately saw an old man sitting on the couch smoking a cigar. The owner of the house wanted to witness the clearing, so we all sat in the living room and asked the ghost a few questions. He answered that he had lived in the house for many years and at the end of his life he had been an alcoholic. He had not been able to see the white light tunnel to the other side. I learned that if a person is not on or at least close to their soul path at the end of their life, either the white light does not appear or they cannot see it, and they fail to enter it. The ghost-spirit then remains on Earth in a different dimension than the living. Falling away from one's light path often happens because of alcohol or drug abuse, having been nasty or cruel to others; and generally the absence of love in one's life. Unfortunately this leaves many spirits Earth-bound until such time as they are guided to the tunnel. As a spirit accepts and absorbs love energy, its vibration changes from dark to light allowing it access to the light tunnel. The ghost in this case insisted on having the owner of the house ask sternly for him to leave. He wanted to be sure that she was releasing him. After this, he was willing to go. We projected love and joy to him, and then asked him to turn around and advance toward the tunnel. He had become quite happy and then he ascended.

Next Tyler and I were intuitively led to the stairway. As we climbed the stairs we felt a female presence, one that was powerful and demanding. She asked us to leave and we said no, that the owner of the house had invited us and we were staying. She was wearing a white dressing gown and certainly behaved as though she was the matriarch of the house. She told us that the present owner did not keep the house properly; it wasn't clean enough or tidy enough. We then cleared her in a similar fashion as the others before her. The owner of the house told us later that she had felt the presence of the matriarchal ghost, and had the impression that she was always annoyed with her. There was a mass of spirits in the basement, who needed to be shown the light, and we released those as well.

The interesting part was when I went outside. Tyler was already hiking up the hill towards the forest following the negative energy. While still in the backyard, I felt the presence of a mighty Native male ghost. He told me he was the chief's son. He had been away on a hunting expedition with three men from his tribe. Upon their return, he found that his small tribe had been murdered by fourteen soldiers who had taken refuge in the nearby forest. This happened long before the house had been built. He told me of his revenge on the soldiers, as we walked up the path toward Tyler and the forest. Tyler and I sat in meditation as the chief's son remorsefully recounted his portrayal complete with telepathic photos and videos. Shadowed in the dark of night, the Native hunting group had found and killed the soldiers one or two at a time, leaving each soldier's body on display in a spine-chilling posture. He showed us one hung from a tree in a grove, another stabbed and left in a depression in the earth in front of a prominent tree, and two blatantly stuffed into the crotches of another pronounced tree. They had painted and dressed the soldier's bodies to reflect the members of their tribe who had been murdered. This left the remaining soldiers in such fear and increasing anxiety particularly at nightfall that they couldn't sleep a wink. These soldiers were terrorized to the point where they became insane just before they were murdered. After the chief's son had finished his confession, Tyler and I simultaneously and excitedly recounted to each other our own version of the man's story; we described the photos, finished each other's sentences and each added to the others' understanding of the disclosure. We each had received the same information! It was truly remarkable that the hunter could project his report to both of us at the same time. Neither Tyler nor I had any judgment against any of the participants. Perhaps this is why the hunter thought he could trust us with his report. We released each of the remaining spirits, soldiers and Native people alike, all into the light tunnel. About two weeks after the clearing, the owner of the house and her son-in-law confided to me that they both felt relieved and comfortable in the house and throughout the property and were especially happy that the woman upstairs had been released.

I was doing a reading for a woman whose house had been for sale for six months during which many people had viewed it, but she had not been presented any offers. She asked me to clear her house. During the clearing, I was shown a barn close to the house, where a miserable ghost was living. He had been visiting the woman's house nightly. After sending him light for a few minutes, he started to become more positive; he confessed to me that he had been harassing the woman's son, and sucking energy from her husband. He told me of whispering in my client's ear just before she awoke every morning, influencing her to believe that she loved the house and didn't want to sell it. He did not want to have to live with another family because he was quite comfortable with the present one. He was afraid of change. He was dressed in farm clothes and he seemed to be from the late 1800's. He wanted to tell me his story.

He told me that he had been married to a woman whom he loved dearly. He was unable to express his feelings of love to her during their time together before she died in childbirth. The baby had also passed away and he was beside himself with grief and remorse. He had lost his own farm due to harsh weather and his depressed state which led to his inability to complete the chores. His farm fell into a state of disrepair and bankruptcy. He was pressed for money so he found employment at another farm close by. He worked there for almost a year but had quit in the autumn, having decided to move to a new town. He began his journey but had been delayed for several reasons and was still travelling when early winter weather enveloped him. He became lost and couldn't find his way to the new town. He found an abandoned shack where he settled planning to wait out the winter. There were a few bottles of alcohol in the shack. One night he drank a lot, wandered from the shack and died of hypothermia close to where the barn now stood. He showed me how cruel he had been to his horse; he was such a sorry sight to see. By the time he died, he was so miserable and had so much hatred in him, that he could not see his light tunnel.

After I cleared him, I looked for the horse. I had until this point never cleared an animal. The horse was lying outside, where the back of the house was now located. I spoke to the horse and he responded. He reasoned through his low self-esteem that he had been mistreated because he didn't deserve any better. He seemed as depressed as his owner had been. I told him he deserved to be happy and free. I projected love to him. Slowly but surely, he stood up and as soon as he realized his owner had vanished, he shot like a sparkly cannonball on a 45 degree angle in the most dazzling display of glittering light, moving at lightning speed all the way to the other side! It was the most spectacular departure I have ever witnessed. When I relayed this information to my client, she confirmed all of the effects on herself and her family. When I talked about the barn, she relayed that the property did not have a barn. When I pressed her about any out buildings, she said there were none. This confused me but finally she said, "Well, there is a barn on the property next door only a stone's throw away from our house." She then explained that her house was built only three years prior. It was located on one acre of land that was severed from the original 100 acre farm.

Many people explain to me that their house could not possibly be haunted because it has been newly built. This is a fallacy, as ghosts often exist for many centuries and don't care when a house was built. Just like you or me, they will eagerly move into a new house.

I spent some time at a friend's farm and found the Native energies were very strong. One day my son said he was feeling a lot of sadness during his visit there. The next time I dropped in, I meditated on the energy of the land. Presently I saw a line-up of about 30 Native people of all ages and genders, and they were all looking at me quietly and patiently, waiting for me to open the light tunnel. They were dressed in their traditional clothing. I spent several hours talking to them and releasing them into the light one by one. They told me of how their tribe had been attacked by white men, and they had been massacred. They showed me some scenes that they had endured. Terrible, unspeakable things had happened. There was a lot of anger, sadness and grief that they conveyed to me. Once released, they were very happy to be away from the place of pain and suffering and on their way to an eternal life of joy. I learned that when someone has the ability to release ghost spirits to the light, ghosts will appear to that person with hope that they can be helped.

It seemed for a while that every week or so a new experience would emerge. I was at a restaurant with my parents one evening. The restaurant had been converted from a residential house that had been built and owned by my great, great grandfather. It was really amazing to see how he as a carriage maker had created a beautiful homestead for his family. My mom remembered visiting her grandparents there when she was a young child. When I went to the ladies' room, a young woman ghost appeared to me and asked me if I could help her. She was agitated and asked if I could hurry. She looked around apprehensively, and exclaimed that I had to release her before the nasty ghost returned as he would block her escape. I sent her courage and love and the light tunnel opened and she rose upward. I felt very grateful that I was able to help ghosts travel to their rightful place on the other side. She was also very grateful and told me so. Similar to the others who had been cleared before her, she filled me with love and appreciation once she had crossed over.

The angels and I have cleared many houses, offices, and properties and guided many ghost-spirits to the other side. I feel distressed when I hear of ghosts who are whisked away from homes by using incomplete clearing methods such as smudging. The method of smudging uses selected dried herbs, usually sage to shoo away unwanted spirits. It evicts the ghost out of its home, neglecting to release it to the other side. This creates homeless ghosts who are moved on from place to place and forced to find yet another home to exist in while they continue their spirit life on earth. I feel sad when I hear people say that they have a ghost in their house, but they like having it there, so they refuse to have it cleared. This only prolongs a spirit's dejected and depressed state. It is much kinder to allow them their freedom to find peace and love on the other side. Some people have told me that their ghost is a friendly ghost and that it likes living in the house with them. I have yet to find any ghost spirit that would rather stay here than go to the light tunnel. Once they feel the love it provides they are filled with joy and they eagerly ascend. Nirvana or heaven is where they belong, and it is our duty to help these misplaced spirits find their way home. When they make themselves known to you they are asking for help, otherwise they would remain silent and unseen.

CHAPTER 6

CONNECTION TO MOTHER EARTH

Many times I have been asked to trust. I will get messages to do something that I would not normally do, and I am to trust that Spirit and the angels will keep me safe and guide me through certain learning situations. Sometimes this information comes through a meditation and sometimes it is physical action I am required to do. I would often be guided on spiritual excursions designed to strengthen my connection to Mother Earth. A strong force would create within me the compelling desire to get in the car and start driving. I would be guided along roads with specific directions such as, "turn left at the next corner, right at the 3rd Line" and so on. Before long, I would usually figure out to which hiking trail or meditation spot they were guiding me. Sometimes it seemed as though the angels were driving the car for me; they are very safe drivers! There were many hiking paths to choose from located close to my house and I was always steered to the one that would suit my learning best.

One of the paths in particular that I was often guided to had a bridge over a river with a swiftly flowing current. I would be guided to go into a light meditation while sitting on the bridge, the rippling water being instrumental in whatever I was being taught at the time. For instance, a negative thought or habit that needed to be released would be brought to my attention. I would be asked to pick a wild flower and then pick off the petals one by one and throw them into the stream as I released each specific aspect of the thought or habit I was eliminating. It was quite effective in discharging negativity as there was a physical facet involved.

A common theme that occurred was my receiving a very quick glimpse of a scenario of a past life in the vicinity where I was visiting. One recurring scene was of Native life-time from long ago. I would see villages of tepees and the magnificent people residing within. It lasted only an instant; just long enough for me to see everything clearly and precisely and to absorb the full sensation of how exceptional it was to live there. I felt so much at home and had a huge sentiment of belonging.

The first delightful jaunt I went on happened at the beginning of my education about intuition. I had recently received a birthday card with a beautiful picture of fireflies on it. I had previously seen three or four fireflies during the summers at the cottage, but had not seen one for several years. I remember wishing I could see some more. A few weeks later I had a strong urge to take my dog for a walk. Usually during the evening I would only stay on the sidewalk and stroll through the subdivision. This particular night I was unquestionably drawn to walk in the nearby field and lost all track of time. I felt compelled to go toward and sit at a place where I had been a few times before. It was dusk, so I thought I would only stay for a short while. I sat on my favourite rock and closed my eyes to take in all the sounds of the crickets and the sweet smells of the wildflowers, and to feel my surroundings better. My dog was sniffing the ground and entertaining herself, always mindful of staying close by my side, so I sat there in deep thought for quite a while. To my utter amusement, when I opened my eyes I saw thousands of glowing fireflies. They were flitting to and fro, flashing high and low, swooping near and far, creating an enchanting display of lights. It was such a magnificent performance illuminating the whole area. I remained on my perch awestruck by the entrancing sight. I was witnessing one of nature's most spectacular and unusual species in multitudes. I thanked the angels for guiding me to this wonderful place and for manifesting my desire to see fireflies. It was a night I will always remember.

Another time, I was driving home from a friend's house at midnight and I was asked by my angels to hike in a familiar forest. Up until this point I had never even had the notion of hiking at midnight. I felt obliged to park the car and stride into the forest. As it was a spontaneous outing, I had no flashlight but mercifully the moon light was bright enough for me to see just my next step. I was unnerved at first, but the angels reminded me that one of my fears that needed to be overcome was being outside in the dark. They assured me that I was just as safe, if not more safe at night by myself as I was during the daytime with unknown risks including dogs, people and bicycles whizzing by. Besides all this, I was told that I was on a required learning mission. It was a beautiful, cool, crisp autumn night, and soon I felt very safe and one with Mother Earth. It was astonishing how the sounds, smells and sensations of nature permeated my being to the core when I was not distracted with the frequently overpowering sense of sight. I had been along that path many times during the day, but this was a totally exhilarating and unique experience. The path looked and felt so dissimilar to its usual appearance; it seemed as if I had never been along it before. In a short time I realized that this exercise was to remind me that I don't need to see any more than a very short distance ahead. The next step in my spiritual journey is all I need to see. It taught me to not be distracted or concerned by attempting to look too far ahead and figure everything out all at once which I had been doing of late. As I need to see, I will be shown and I am to follow along the path with faith and trust alone. I saw numerous insights that night about my life in general and about past lives as a Native person and of travelling on foot at night. I received answers to questions I had recently been asking about as well. I arrived back at my car so touched by the safety I felt from the angel's care. I have taken many strolls in the dark since, and even sitting outside at night devoid of ambient light brings a greater awareness than during the day.

One particular winter day, I was asked if I was ready to learn some very important lessons. As always, when the angels asked me this question, I replied favourably. I was guided to a familiar park and shown an ascending trail that I was to follow. The trail ended at an entrance to a cavern. I saw that the floor of the cave was completely covered in a one-foot thick layer of very slippery glistening ice. I was advised to traverse the cave which was on a fairly steep uphill grade and meditate on a rock at the other end. I could see that the rock I was to sit on was also covered with glimmering slick ice. It would be challenging at best to sit still on the rock, never mind to focus on meditation. It was an impossible feat to accomplish in my limited human perception. I angrily refused, telling them that it was too dangerous and this had been a big waste of time. I turned around intending to walk back to the car, but I received such a strong undeniable urge to carry on with the original purpose of the trek. My guides promised me that they would hold me up safely, and that no harm would come to me. I resisted for a while but finally gave in, with the notion that at the first tiny slip on the ice, I would immediately return to the car. I said to my angels, "Alright, do you promise to keep me absolutely safe?" Immediately I heard, "Of course we will, trust us!" I took a big breath and launched my first step toward the rock. I felt several angels on each side of me holding me up and one in front pulling me forward over the ice. I could not have had an easier time traversing the cave even if I had been walking nonchalantly on a dry summer day. I arrived at the rock and sat on it comfortably and securely, being held safely by my angels. I had a very amazing meditation about learning to trust my angels. They said they will always keep me safe and on my soul path. I asked, "What if it's my soul path for me to fall and hurt myself?" They replied that they would have to allow me to fall in that case, but they would make sure that I didn't hurt myself any more than was necessary for my soul learning. While sitting on the rock, I also had a very important vision presented to me. It answered a lot of questions I had been asking recently, and gave me direction as to my future and the decisions I would be making very soon.

As I left the cave, still supported and safe, I felt very blessed that I had these powerful and helpful beings to assist me in my life. We are on Earth for a physical existence and learning through physical experiences has much more clout than would otherwise be possible. The angels could have guided me through a meditation while I sat safely in the comfort of my home with the purpose of increasing my trust in them. However, the actual experience of the cave adventure was not only exhilarating but also a brilliant exercise that bonded the angels and me together forever.

I am often guided to sit or stand with my back against a specific tree such as the tree that I subsequently named "Grandfather Tree." 'He' was a magnificent sugar maple tree not far from my home. As I stood alongside of the trunk, I immediately felt his dynamic presence radiating through me. The vibration reminded me of a wise First Nations Elder. Energy emanating from Grandfather Tree was so calming, that whenever I became upset, I would go to this tree and he would soothe my nerves and bring a deep peacefulness within me. Grandfather Tree became one of my favourite trees that I visited often. He also became one of the teaching trees for attendees of my workshops. Grandfather Tree always gave strong and helpful energy to each of my students. There were many trees that I was steered to including the Tree of Knowledge. When I stood with my back to this tree I would sense large amounts of energy absorbing into me. I was not always aware of specific information but was told that the energy permeated within me and would be revealed when the time was right. I would usually be advised that I needed to return within a few days, when I would receive the next blast of knowledge that was required for my spiritual learning. The Tree of Grounding was very helpful for me too, and I often stopped just for a minute to stand beside it while I was out with my horse. Sometimes I was directed to ride my bike to the tree and sit at the base for a while. I could sense a strong grounding force hugging me into Mother Earth much as a magnet would. Many times I needed this powerful grounding energy to keep me focused and secure on my spiritual journey.

Many times I have witnessed artistically detailed pictures in the clouds. One day I saw an anchor which came with a channelled message that I needed to be more grounded, and that certain people and especially my horse were helping to anchor my energy into the ground. I was informed that some day when I was ready to expand my connection to horses I would see my horse, Jack, in the clouds. About four months later, I was hiking and stopped to take a drink of water. I peered up into the sky and there was a perfect rendition of Jack, so complete and detailed that a skilled artist would have trouble creating such precision. It was an exact replica including his few white hairs on his nose and two white ankle socks on his hind legs and his expression of unconditional love in his perfectly duplicated eyes. I stared in awe for a while, until it was whisked away by the wind.

Another time I was swimming and looked up to the sky and saw as clear as day, a dachshund with a large heart on her back. A second dog was standing on her back, with its front legs perched on the heart and its nose pointing upward to the heavens. My dachshund named Heidi had passed away about two years prior to this sighting. There was a very comforting feeling that accompanied this cloud picture, with the insinuation that Heidi was planning on returning to me as a fluffy white square-shaped dog. She had previously indicated to me that she wanted to return to me in this lifetime. I felt that this was an explicit communication for a purpose that will eventually be revealed.

Many times I have realized messages in the form of hearts. Heart shapes came to me in formations in clouds, rocks, puddles, spilled liquids, shadows, hoof prints, tea leaves and in dust or snow. Strings or elastics would fall on the floor that twisted in the shape of a heart. I would sometimes find fifteen hearts or more per day in very creative and diverse displays. When I discovered the hearts it was at a point in my life when my heart was closed down. These hearts were clear indications that it was crucial for me to change my ways; to become open-hearted. Frequently after already seeing many hearts in one day, I would have a good "hearty" laugh when yet another one appeared.

I developed a captivating connection to Mother Earth especially through trees, water, night sky, clouds and sunlight. One day, I was riding Jack through a familiar forest path and suddenly beside us was Jesus riding on a white mare. Jesus had only come to me very rarely previously and only when I was beside myself with emotional pain and praying profusely. I was surprised and happy to see Him. He asked me to follow Him to a tree. He called it the Tree of Ascension. I dismounted and stood beside the tree and it felt much more highly vibrational than any other tree I had ever felt. Jesus said I was to go there whenever I was given the intuition to do so. I consequently spent many afternoons riding my bike or walking to the forest and meditating at the base of this spectacular tree. I was guided to take my sons there and a couple of my friends and clients. We would obtain advice and messages from the tree and most of all; strong vibrations that had no word content, but were very powerful nonetheless. About six months after my first visit to the tree, I rode Jack there and stood beside the tree still mounted. It was winter and Jack's hooves started to slip on the roots of the tree. Falling off in slow motion and unable to prevent it, I landed on the ground under Jack's ribcage. He was able to right himself once he was relieved of my weight. He turned and looked at me, moved his hooves very carefully to avoid my body parts, then bent his head toward my face and gently nuzzled my cheek. I laughed out loud as he tickled my face. Slowly I stood, observing the details of the scene and remounted. It was a very strange happening as I stepped on the same tree roots and they were not slippery. Jack had not slid once on the snow that day. I was very curious as to how and why this happened and it kept repeating in my thoughts. Two days later, I was having lunch with my son in Toronto. After we finished eating and stood up to walk out of the restaurant I looked for the first time at the painting that was hanging on the wall above our table. My jaw almost dropped to the floor as my son said in a concerned tone, "Mom what's wrong?"

The painting was the exact replica of my recent fall. There was a woman with brown hair lying on the ground beside a large deciduous tree with another similar large tree beside it. The scene was right at the edge of a forest. Her bay horse with two hind white socks was standing right above her, nuzzling her face with the reins hanging down on the ground. There was a page wire fence that ran along the far side of the trees leading to a corner in the fence dividing two fields, and another field beyond going up a hill. The sun was shining in the exact same angle and through the leaves, virtually identical to how it had been when I fell. I was stunned. Here we were at what we thought was a randomly chosen restaurant in the large city of Toronto far away from where I lived, standing in front of a perfectly detailed rendition of my incident two days before! I don't believe in coincidences, so I knew there was a message involved. I kept asking to be shown the meaning of the episode. Finally I was told that I was "falling at the feet of Jesus," the tree representing Jesus, meaning that I must surrender to Him completely in order to ascend to my next level of enlightenment. As usual there were other various personal messages following the main one.

CHAPTER 7

SURRENDER

There were a few times when I was guided to surrender to my Higher Power. The first such time was during a very wearisome chain of events that led to a serious illness. I had become very weak and fatigued over the previous months. One night around nine o'clock during a severe episode, I called a friend of mine who was a nurse at the hospital in town. She was very concerned and told me that if the symptoms did not subside by midnight, I was to call 911 and she would meet me in the emergency department. Later that night as I lay in bed helpless and too weak to move, I realized that I did not have the strength to walk over to where the phone was located. Even if I did, I knew the ambulance would not find me, as my apartment was tucked away in the back of a house out in the country in the middle of a forest. When I gave my friends and clients detailed directions, they often could not find my place. I was very ill and was close to death. As I lay there, I became aware that I was mentally drifting off to a state I had never experienced before. On my would-be death-bed I was so weak that my only option was to surrender fully to my Higher Power.

I felt as if I was not present in my body anymore, and that I could easily fade away into oblivion. I silently said to God, "If it is your will for me to die tonight, I'm ok with that. I surrender to you." I descended into a deep meditative state. Immediately I was spiritually whisked away to visit my sons. One lived in Toronto and the other in London. I saw each one and felt that I was right there with them. I was shown how they would react to my death. I also saw how their lives would be lived out in my absence. I observed that they would be sad at first, but would ultimately recover, and that they would each have a happy and fulfilling existence. I even saw their wives and children and pets that they would have in the future. I felt satisfied that they would be well and happy. Next I was jettisoned away to my other family members and close friends, and even to my horse. I saw a very quick version of how their lives would play out and how they would thrive and carry on without me. I was shown my horse living at my friend's farm, being ridden by nice and kind people and living a good and happy life. I felt satisfied that all would be well. I was ready to leave Earth *if* that was the higher plan.

I became weaker and fell into an even deeper state of consciousness. Presently I saw a very bright light above my head and then other similar but smaller lights began to surround me. There were 12 altogether. I did not count them I just knew intrinsically how many there were. I knew they had either come to heal me or to help me transfer to the other side. They were so full of love and light and I was entirely and utterly comforted, supported and happy. They stayed with me for a while, how long I do not know, and soon I sensed myself floating. I felt as if I was floating in an ocean of unconditional love so complete and so full of peace, joy, bliss, and tranquillity and immensely full of LOVE. I felt like I was in heaven, floating in Creator's love. Eventually I could feel and see all the molecules in my body, starting with my skin, leaving my body one by one and dissipating into the sea of love. Layer by layer my body was absorbed into the sea as if I was a sugar cube melting into a cup of water. Finally I became totally one with love and I no longer existed as me. I had become one with All There Is. It is challenging for me to explain the beauty and the depth of what I felt, saw and heard. I have no idea how long this went on for, and eventually I fell into a very deep, restful sleep.

The next thing I remember was waking up and looking at the clock. It was midnight on the dot. I quickly took inventory of how I felt, and ... I felt good, much better than I had for many weeks. My symptoms had ceased at least for the moment. I was extremely grateful that I was alive and well. The next day, still weak from my condition, my friend took me to the doctor. More tests and procedures were scheduled to discover the cause of my ailments.

I rested as much as I could over the following weeks and gained strength, knowing that I was mending, but not yet cured. About six weeks later I had another episode. This bout was different from the other times. I was in pain and nauseated and felt faint and dizzy. I felt the cause of my condition being flushed out of my body. Up till that point no doctor or health care professional had determined the cause of my problems. Exhausted, I lay back down in bed to rest for the night. Suddenly a very loud and masterful male voice proclaimed: **"NOW YOU ARE HEALED."** My bed shook with the mighty heavenly vibration. I can only tell you that I knew it was God. It was spoken with such commanding authority. The immense love I felt was exceptionally overwhelming and encompassing. I lay still for a long time trying to regain my bearings. Then I barely managed to utter, "ok, thanks" in the smallest whisper possible. I knew I had been healed by some awesome power, and that my physical ailments had been transformed into health.

CHAPTER 8

ANCHORS OF ANGER

As I was driving to my friend's cottage one day, I had an unprovoked immense feeling of anger overwhelm me. It was induced within me by my angels, as I had not recently had any cause to become angry. It was necessary for me to experience this emotion in order for me to release old anger that I was still carrying from my past. Angels are very adept at triggering within us certain negative moods and sentiments for the purpose of releasing them, using them as learning opportunities, so we can move forward on our light path. Anger along with other negative emotions is a trigger that informs you that you have work to do; to release negative energy within yourself and replace it with love. Once I arrived at the cottage, I meditated on anger. The following was channelled through me and I was asked to include them in my writings.

Ego-mind Justifications for Anger

I was retaining fear through anger for protection, because of the notion that releasing anger would permit me to be vulnerable. If I had a flash of anger stored within myself just under the surface ready to attack, I would be able to defend myself against similar energy, or even mount a counter attack. Anger was my defence armour and would prevent people from taking advantage of me. This way I could retain my ego-based self-respect.

Many relationships are controlled through fear. Control through anger is used as a very common threat in families, as well as with leaders of institutions and countries to dominate their members and constituents. Control through fear only lasts as long as the victim allows his fear to rule him. Once the victim overcomes or confronts the fear, the controller no longer has the upper hand and the relationship is revised. Similarly a revolution may occur or a change in government in a country where the population has either conquered their fear of suppression or are at least willing to retaliate despite their fear.

The ego-mind relates its fear of being vulnerable to being in danger. The ego wants to be constantly in control. When the ego-mind feels vulnerable in any situation for instance, losing command, it goes into fear mode; anger or some similar negative emotion then erupts. When anger is present, the ego-mind feels that it has regained control, and is no longer vulnerable. The ego-mind will use life circumstances to keep creating more fear/anger instead of allowing itself to be vulnerable.

The ego-mind thinks that love equals vulnerability. If there is anger within, love can quickly and easily be pushed away. This is often displayed through dysfunctional behaviour. If a lover becomes too intense, the person feels trapped or cramped within the relationship because he is unable to accept the amount of love being offered. The person can show distain for the other through anger and push the lover away far enough until he regains comfort in his own space again. It is a defence against too much love for a limited level of acceptance.

Anger is very devastating to the body, mind and soul. Like attracts like which means that anger requires a similar energy to attach itself to. Lashing back in anger to someone who is infuriated, can provoke a huge spiral of rage. Anger opposing anger creates multiples of negative energy, inducing negative feelings between people that can last a lifetime.

Freedom of Love

After receiving the above information I asked: "What are the anchors of love?" I was given the following information. Love is never binding or controlling so it could not be called anchors of love. Love is freely given and freely received; therefore I called it freedom of love.

Know that there is no such thing as vulnerability when living in a state of love. It is much more powerful to react with love, because then no negativity can touch you. When you face an angry person, and send them love, their anger recedes and disappears, as it has nothing to anchor itself into. Vibrationally, an angry person's negative energy output is deflected off of the love energy of the other person's aura. Because there is nothing to attach to, the anger bounces back to the angry person. When projected irritation is redirected back, the angry one reacts with surprise as the habitual or pre-conceived expectation of a fight or argument has not been met. This is a distraction from the usual argumentative routine and fury disperses. Potentially volatile situations can dissipate easily and quickly when love opposes anger. When one gives way to love, and anger dissolves, it is so empowering for all the people involved. It is wonderfully surprising when the situation dissolves right in front of your eyes.

When living in a state of love, you are very well protected from fear. Love is *always* much more powerful than fear. Living in fear opens you up to more dark or negative energy through the Law of Attraction. A person living even part-time in negativity and darkness is vulnerable, while his counterpart, living full-time in love and light is not. People who project love to others instead of fear create a very strong bond and can thereby develop a very kind, respectful, and reciprocal relationship which leads to Divine or Whole relationships.

A powerful way to bring light into yourself is to visualize light from the Universal Light Source coming down and filling your whole being including your aura. This brings all of the positive aspects of the universe: joy, peace, serenity, freedom, illumination, bliss, kindness, giving, and all good things to you. Fill yourself with this light every morning before you get up, at night before you fall asleep, and as often as you can during the day. Live in constant mindfulness that you are one with your Higher Power. As well as bringing joy, this process will start to expose all negativity that needs to be released in your life. That is one of the collective soul purposes we are here to learn and remember. By surrounding yourself with love-light, you are able to shine your light to others. Others will see your light through their spiritual eye; it is natural and subliminal. It feeds your whole spirit through the conscious and the subconscious. Others will aspire to become as you are. It is a spiritual out-pouring of love, joy and kindness to others. You can project this love-light to people who are ill, or unhappy, or you can send it to your workplace, your church, a hospital, a jail, the world and so forth. If everyone did this, the world would become much more peaceful and humane. To accomplish this, visualize the people you want to help as a hologram in front of you, feeding them with the love in your heart, see them completely covered with white light. For buildings, visualize them being filled with white healing light inside and out. For the world, see the Earth as a globe and cover it with white light. Doing this for a few minutes will send love and compassion to all within.

CHAPTER 9

CREATION OF OUR EARTH JOURNEY

Before our lives begin on Earth, much thought and energy is spent on creating the perfect life for the soul. The soul has a specific agenda to fulfil in order to learn what is necessary to climb its ladder of enlightenment. All worldly goods are left behind when a body expires and the soul goes to the other side/ Nirvana/ Heaven. The only thing that is transferred from this life to the afterlife is the amount of enlightenment that the soul was able to achieve in this lifetime. Unfortunately there are many people who don't understand this very simple and obvious concept and they spend much of their precious time pursuing the almighty dollar and material security, ignoring their soul's quiet persistent quest for spiritual progress.

Souls come to Earth to learn as much as they can; lifetime after lifetime, they come here to learn the whole plan of what is available. This is why lifetimes may be filled with negative aspects, events and experiences to deal with including negative karma. People of western origin may refer to this concept as "what goes around comes around." Many eastern religions believe that karma created in the past, including past lives, is carried with you into your present life. One of the common life purposes of all souls is to release negative karma, along with as much other negativity as possible. By releasing this darkness, people open up space to absorb more light from Higher Power, thereby climbing the ladder of en-light-enment.

Much negative karma is created within relationships, and is thus released through relationships. The following are some simplified examples. Negative karma is produced from mistreating people through abuse and cruelty, and basically from treating people or animals and all things with anything less than love and compassion. Many souls chose to come to Earth in this particular lifetime to take advantage of the volatile Earth energies. These help to release negative karma much more quickly than ever before in the history of Earth. All karma must be released before ascension. Those on their path will attract opportunities to release karma. Often this happens in rapid consecutive events generating close to intolerable circumstances. Frequently a person has constructed a span of time during their life for the release of karmic debt during their life-creation stage with their council. Karmic release can be recognized in some of the following: relationship break-ups, grieving the death of a loved one, emotional trauma, physical dis-ease or syndrome, serious accident, eating disorders, financial hardship, mental upset or illness and career dilemmas. They may happen singularly or several at the same time. They are predominantly emotionally challenging and may include physical, mental and spiritual aspects as well.

After an intense karmic release comes the Karmic Healing phase. Karmic Healing is the recovery time subsequent to an episode of profound karmic release. Often dis-ease manifests because of long-term stress in the person and can be recognized as an illness or condition. In such a case, it could be displayed as mental, emotional or physical breakdown or an upset, burnt out demeanour or sheer exhaustion. The person may heal alone, or there may be a specific person or people who will help to facilitate the healing. This designated healer could be a therapist, nurse, business partner, a friend, family member or a care-giver. Karmic Healing requires the liberating of one's self from the thoughts, words, actions and habits of the self-imposed incarceration of the karmic relationship. If a new relationship is entered before the healing is complete, the person will find himself attracted to, and unwittingly creating, a similar relationship to the one he's trying to heal from. Once the karmic healing is finished, the person is free to enter into the next phase of the soul journey. Many times this next stage is a spiritual path which embraces many spiritual gifts representing rewards for having completed a key chapter in one's life.

A key point here is to do your best to not create any more negative karma for yourself. This is simply accomplished by being kind, respectful, generous, forgiving and generally treating all others and yourself with love while keeping firm healthy boundaries. This enables you to continue rapidly on your spiritual path, reducing the time spent or wasted on having to release newly created negative karma.

Creating the soul's next lifetime is an intricate process. The soul along with its wise council decides what it needs to learn, and arranges the life accordingly. This council is made up of wise elders who are light beings. They possess all the information necessary to help the soul choose everything it will be and everything that will happen in its lifetime. The same council remains with the soul for many lifetimes and knows what is best for that particular soul. Together the council and the soul choose its parents, siblings, partners, spouses, friends, gender, location of birth and subsequent living locations, appearance of the body, any handicaps or challenges, temperament, financial situations, religion, pets, sports, hobbies, events, schools, vocation, jobs and so on. They make decisions on everything that is important. These decisions help to create the personality and conditions that will allow the most learning for the soul. They help the soul to choose a general plan of several choices to be selected from once they are here. Prospective parents and siblings have the choice to accept or deny a soul's request to be part of their family. As each soul's plan must also fit into everyone else's plan, it may take a lot of intricate design to arrange a life. Often the council warns the soul that its current plan has included too many challenges and will put too much stress on its future person. The council frequently suggests easier options and fewer challenges. It is the soul's prerogative to modify the life plan to the advice of the council or to adhere to its original choices. Many souls pack their lives so full of activities that too many distractions are generated. Its human aspect has great difficulty in processing events favourably for the planned learning.

Once everyone is satisfied that the plan is suitable, it is then taken to the soul's Higher Power for input, examination, discussion and finally endorsement. The soul is then shown its proposed life-events in a hologram. Important segments in the soul's future life are shown over and over with all possible deviations so the soul will react constructively to any of the variations should they arise. The soul is prepped to recognize the situation as important just before or as it arrives. This can sometimes be an eerie feeling that something negative is about to happen and it can be the tensing of muscles just before a physical action is required, or a calming of the mind when a clear mental decision must be made quickly. Often after such situations there may be a sentiment that there was a supernatural occurrence. That could include super-fast thinking and reacting, or a sudden burst of extra strength being expended.

Déjà vu is the soul's tracking device. It demonstrates

to the soul that it is on target. Déjà vu means 'already seen.' It is a strange unexpected feeling that one has been in the exact place and time before and yet there is no recollection of having been there physically. It is a strong and undeniable incident that only lasts for a few seconds, but is inexplicably significant. It feels as if time stands still or ceases to exist for a short while. Specific settings for déjà vu are planned and experienced in the hologram during preparation for the life. They are prearranged at a time and location when the person experiencing the phenomenon is able to register it in his mind. That's why it usually feels good and exciting from a deep level when déjà vu occurs.

Soul groups are collections of souls that have similar vibrations and are on similar missions. A soul may choose to incarnate with others in his soul group located close by. They may be family members, neighbours, co-workers or friends. Soul mates give enormous support to each other. This is important especially if one or both souls are on challenging journeys. Some souls incarnate with people from neighbour-ing soul groups which also give good provision. Two people may meet who have never met before in this lifetime, yet they have a strong sense that they have known each other previously. This is soul recognition, and is meant to attract attention. It may be a brief encounter at a workshop or restaurant with the two knowing they will never meet again. This leaves each person with an underlying notion of satisfaction and sense of encouragement that there are others on Earth with the same purpose as themselves. On the other hand, an introduction of two soul mates could lead to them becoming friends, lovers, spouses or partners that could last a short time or a lifetime. Each person in the soul group has his own purpose and a good proportion of that purpose is to further the level of enlightenment for the soul group as a whole. Neighbouring soul groups also help to propel each other up the ladder of enlightenment. The soul's purpose is to bring in as much light as possible into itself. This promotes and projects love to others, thereby simultaneously helping others up their ladder of enlightenment.

Reincarnation

According to the soul, the best way to describe life is "you get in, do your purpose, and then you get out." It is a mission. When you are finished your Earth life and you are on the other side, you are debriefed. You evaluate everything that you did while on Earth and decide what you still need to do. Then you return to life on Earth, do your work and leave again. There is not a whole lot of purpose or motivation for the soul to continue life on Earth once its purpose is finished. Most people leave fairly soon after their purpose is complete. This is why often we know someone who has just achieved what the human side of us would think of as a huge goal, and very soon after, the person passes away. Many of us think it is such a shame that that person didn't have time to enjoy her newly found higher human status, but in soul reality, she accomplished exactly what she was here to do. To remain with no further purpose could be considered as what it would be like to keep repeating grade three over and over and over.

Another reason why people leave Earth is if they are not heading in the right direction of their soul path. After repeated attempts by the Higher Power to improve the situation, the person is allowed to leave in order to re-group and start again. Often many exits are included in a lifetime. An exit is an opportunity to leave this life earlier than the final exit. Often it involves having a short visit to the other side, recalibrating and then returning to Earth for a new life. If someone is diagnosed with a terminal or painful disease, they may choose a quick exit such as an accident instead of prolonging the agony and suffering. Exits are sometimes integrated into a life as a choice, after a major challenge has occurred. There is a reasonable amount of time given for the person to recuperate. If the person cannot overcome the challenge, and is not able to continue on his planned soul path, as a last resort, an exit can be taken if it is sanctioned.

News of a loved one's death or any surprising news may be received as a shock, because the ego-mind is not privy to the information that the soul has. Our souls know all there is to know about the Universe, or can get access to it through many sources including the Higher Self. The ego-mind is formed freshly for each lifetime, and therefore has no previous knowledge of life on the other side. We need to delve into our soul intelligence to find this Universal knowledge. An exception is a young child who has retained some memory of life on the other side and may refer to it periodically. As the child ages, the memory usually dissipates.

The Higher Self has access to a cosmic library of sorts that contains all the information available in the Universe. It also stores all the information we need to live our lives according to our light path. It contains all the knowledge that we have accrued during all the lives we have lived. This intelligence is accessed by the Higher Self and is available to you when required. For example, the first time someone tries a sport or game, 'she' may excel surprisingly which is commonly called beginner's luck. What seems to be an innate ability may be attributed to having had a similar experience in a past life. Likewise, in an emergency situation, one may solve a completely foreign problem quickly without thinking, as her Higher

Self is streaming the necessary information to her.

Generally, when a person passes away, a woman for example, there is a specific process her soul partakes in. Immediately upon death, as long as she is on her path, a tunnel of white light will appear. Her guardian angel will escort her up the tunnel when it is the right time for her to ascend. It is a joyous reunion when the soul joins with her guardian angel again! Before a soul ascends up the light tunnel it usually opts to visit its loved ones to say goodbye, and to make sure that they will be alright. When this happens, the receiver is given an encompassing feeling of euphoria and freedom. Empathic people will pick up on this psychic visit and feel the supernatural energy. The passing one sees the remaining life journey of the ones she is leaving behind, which helps her to feel confident that her loved ones, although they will grieve for a while, will eventually thrive. She is then able to leave Earth with the knowledge that all is well, and that her loved ones will continue along their chosen paths.

Once she ascends up the light tunnel, her soul is met by her most loving and closest light being friends. Included are passed loved ones, passed pets, counsellors, angels, archangels and a whole host of loved ones. Her spirit is allowed to return to Earth often to visit her loved ones, and to ensure that they are on the road to recovery after her death; that all grieving is proceeding constructively. She will be able to emanate energy to them, to let them know she is well and that she loves them. Often these visits occur at night while the Earth-bound one is asleep. There are fewer blockages while one's ego-mind is resting, which allows the message to be delivered more easily. Occasionally I hear of visiting souls turning on electrical devices such as lights, alarms, door bells, and helping in various other ways.

Once on the other side, the passed one undergoes the process of observing the hologram of the entire life she just left starting from conception. The hologram plays out her own reactions to life events and how they affected her. She is also shown how other people reacted to her input in all the events of their lives together. The feedback indicates how she affected people both positively and negatively. This procedure can take a relatively short time, or may take many Earth years to complete, depending on how many events and reactions need to be processed. The information derived from this session helps to determine the path that the soul will take in its next lifetime.

It is worthy to note that what is carried over to the other side when one passes generally is the amount of love that has been given, and the amount of love that has been received along with how much one has helped others. This indicates the degree of enlightenment that one achieved in her lifetime. The amount of negative energy that was acquired and projected is subtracted from the previous sum and a level of illumination is determined for the soul. This calculation establishes which spiritual echelon the soul will be residing in until the next life begins. The spiritual level one leaves Earth with is the same level at which one returns with in her next life. There is no provision for measuring the number of material objects that were acquired or how much money was accumulated.

The Path of Ascension

Ascension is when a soul moves upward through the different echelons of Heaven/Nirvana. In between Earth lives, the soul remains in the highest state that it reached during its last life and is housed in a corresponding echelon. Ascension

can be instigated by a single awakening which can be instanta-
neous, or a gradual one that incorporates many steps through
many years. During a meditation my angels took me on a spiritual journey and they showed me the path to ascension.

Suddenly I was taken into a very deep state of consciousness. Immense love, peace and joy were emanating
through me. Presently I felt as if I was going up in an elevator.
I knew I was absorbing lots of knowledge on a subconscious
level, as amazing energy flowed through me and around me.
Consciously I was aware of feeling a powerful vibration. I kept
going up very quickly through thousands of layers of echelons.
Echelons retain increasing light vibration as you rise up. There
is an echelon for each vibration that a soul has reached in its
lifetime. There could be either one soul residing in an echelon
or several souls if they are at the same state of illumination. I
could see and feel many souls around me as I travelled through
their echelons. They were so kind and happy that I was experiencing their "homes" and their existence. They were encour-
aging me every step of the way. I felt so much gratitude and
positivity and unconditional love from them. I finally arrived
at the top where God was waiting for me. He said, "This I have
shown you so you can tell others; that they may also strive
for this. It's like a sneak preview of what is possible. Once you
have it in your awareness and know it exists, it is then attainable." It is reassuring somehow to know that spiritual growth
is regarded with such high esteem and is rewarded on the other side. This newly acquired wisdom filled me with incentive
to work even more zestfully at my spiritual development.

Short Lives

Sometimes a soul's purpose is accomplished in a short
life. It may need to learn only a few lessons to finish a series of

lives so it can advance to a higher calling. Or it may need to experience a childhood death for reasons beyond that which we can understand with our limited human tunnel vision. After a soul had a very challenging recent life, it may need a life full of love and kindness to renew its interest in Earth life, and as an incentive to continue its soul journey. Its soul mates will decide to embark on the mission with it so they will be together. The child will then be comforted by similar energy during its lifetime. This helps the child through its life and death, especially if it has chosen a difficult road to travel. Kind and generous souls which choose to be accomplices, console the child in time of crisis, and lend assistance to each other during the challenging time of grieving. Because of a special connection to another, there may be a specific soul that is most suitable to help and to nurture the child-soul while it learns its requirements for further enlightenment. An example of this is my best friend from childhood, Denise Bebenek and her daughter Meagan. They came to Earth together for a very important mission. Meagan passed away at the age of five because of an inoperable brain tumour. Denise had a vision when she left the hospital the day Meagan passed, and began her journey as the founder "Meagan's Walk: Creating a Circle of Hope". She raises funds for paediatric brain tumour research which is now having global impact on children all over our world.

Frequently people become enveloped in their grief here, and sometimes even blame others or God for their predicament. When the truth is seen during the hologram viewing from the other side, the immense gifts that these souls have given to each other is finally realized.

I had a session with a woman whose grandson had passed away unexpectedly at her home. She was devastated. The incident had occurred several years before, and she was still in the early stages of grieving, unable to get past her guilt and fear. She blamed herself for not being more aware of the situation which ultimately ended her grandson's life. Her angels advised that her grandson's soul path objective was to pass away early in his life to ensure his soul's required learning. Before they came to Earth, the two of them planned to be together through this tragedy. They were to help each other attain that which each of their souls was required to learn. One of the grandmother's purposes was to help the remaining family members cope with the huge loss while they learned their soul lessons. I was shown the grandmother speaking with her council on the other side while planning her life. She was absolutely adamant that she be present in the young boy's life, and especially at the time of his death. She wanted to do as much for him as she could. I could feel her soul's complete unconditional love for his soul. She also had the strength to hold the rest of the family together; she was the perfect candidate for the role she played in this sequence of events. My client was visibly relieved when she heard this information from her angels, and mentioned to me that she had a deep inner sense that the truth had been revealed. She released her guilt with the help of the angels and left with a strong peaceful feeling. I see many scenarios of souls planning their challenging lives, and each time these helpers are so bright, caring and loving. They are so excited to start their life on Earth, oblivious to the pain and suffering they will endure here.

Soul Contracts

Soul Contracts are decided upon and arranged to benefit all concerned. Contracts are designed to create teaching and learning situations that are necessary for each soul's illumination. They may be created to encourage the release of karma, or of negative aspects of one's personality. Once a contract is complete, the people involved are free to advance to their next experience. There is a feeling of relief and closure. Relationships formed for the purpose of this process will dissolve, improve or at least change upon conclusion of the contract.

A client presented her disillusionment about the fact that she took care of her dad who had ALS. For three years, she provided everything he required and spent all her time with him during what she considered to be her prime dating years. Although she was glad that she helped him, she was bitter and convinced that she had missed her opportunity to find Mr. Right. The angels said that she and her dad were engaged in a soul contract. It was her task to take care of him throughout his last years of life, and his function was to accept her support gratefully. Her future husband was from the same soul group as her father. She was incapable of attracting her mate until she acquired the necessary vibration that could only be attained through completion of the soul contract with her dad. We often need to finish off a purpose or soul contract before we can move forward into a more desirable time in our lives. There are as many reasons why we come to live our particular lives as there are people.

When one passes, her soul energy may remain intermittently with loved ones for a while and often for a very long time. The soul travels between Earth and the other side, fulfilling its duties in both places. Eventually when its loved ones on Earth have healed enough, the soul spends the majority of its time on the other side, completing its duties and preparing for its next life. To connect with a past loved one, centre yourself in a quiet place and recreate the heart-felt love that was felt while your beloved was still embodied on Earth.

This fills you with the energy of the recently passed loved one, opening the doorway which encourages that spirit to visit. The soul may visit at that time or may wait for a more suitable time and place to visit.

Often souls postpone their journey up the light tunnel for a while. This may be to help their loved ones adjust to life without them. By remaining on Earth, their energy infuses into their loved ones, giving them comfort through the stages of grieving. As the loved one becomes stronger, the soul will cross over, and visit less often.

The journey through the light tunnel can also be delayed while a soul finishes its learning requirements. This helps to make their hologram session proceed more quickly. What is learned on Earth seems to hold more impact compared to the lessons that are available on the other side. The soul who opts for this type of learning feels that it did not finish its purpose and wants to be more complete before moving on. In this case, a soul stays on Earth for a while to be close to a higher vibrating person. When it has finished its learning, it can absorb that person's high love energy, enabling the soul to find and ascend the light tunnel.

CHAPTER 10

READINGS AND HEALINGS

Eight years ago, and only three weeks before Christmas, I was fired from one of my part-time jobs. I searched for work but was unable to find a suitable office for employment. I worked as a temporary, filling in for health-care providers who were ill, on vacation and who had broken bones from accidents. Work was sporadic and unreliable. As my savings account dwindled, I began looking desperately for another way to create an income. The angels guided and encouraged me to use my intuitive abilities to help others and at the same time help myself by booking fair-exchange appointments with clients. They counselled me on how to do angel readings and eventually other intuitive sessions and channelled healings.

During an angel reading, also known as an akashic record reading, the client's angels, archangels and guides channel information through me with words, pictures, videos and feelings. I speak the words as they come through and I describe the photos and feelings I am given to my clients. Many different angels, archangels and light beings arrive for specific parts of the reading and healing. Most often Archangels Michael, Ariel, Gabriel and Rafael, and St. Germain show up. Sometimes God, Divine Mother, Jesus and the Holy Spirit, Parmahansa Yogananda, Metatron, and countless others come as well.

Angels tell you what you need to know to follow your soul path. They will never tell you what to do, but will describe and clarify the whole picture from all aspects, enabling you to make an informed decision. Angels are always around you. It is their purpose to help you, and they are overtly eager and so excited when you ask for their assistance. They can hardly contain their enthusiasm during the reading. Because of the Law of Free Will, they are only allowed to help at *your* request.

The initial angel reading begins with the angels describing three to six things that they want to help their person with. This can last for half to three quarters of the reading. Often they discuss aspects of the person's life, such as relationships, decisions, finances, past or present lovers, children, parents, spouses, career, health, deceased loved ones, upcoming events and pets. However, the readings have a far-reaching scope and can cover any subject and experience in life. The angels then ask if there are any questions that the client wants to ask. Clients ask questions ranging from anything and everything you could imagine! If clients ask questions about their acquaintances, the angels tune me into them, as well as loved ones who have passed away. Angels adhere to a privacy code and will never reveal information that the person in question would disapprove of. Pets are often discussed and especially if they are displaying any odd behaviours.

Angels do not adhere to Earth-time, so I have dubbed their time-space continuum as 'angel time.' Angels go by events that happen in your life. If someone asks when they will find a great job, the angels will reply with an explanation of perhaps five events that the client has to learn from before they find their dream job. They will also give an approximate number of weeks or months by which time that job might be found.

Angels give information in the present moment. If you change the way you are living your life, your future changes too. Sometimes I see an accident or a difficult time approaching.

The angels will advise their charge, for example a woman client, as to what lessons she needs to learn in order to avoid the catastrophe. If she is destined for a car accident and she learns the lessons only half-way, she may have a fender-bender. If she slows down and focuses more, and learns the lessons very well, she will not need to be taught by experiencing the accident. Instead, on the day the accident was to occur, she may be detoured by taking a wrong turn, or detained by forgetting an item that she needs so she returns home. This will prevent the accident from happening, as the vehicle she was to collide with will be long gone, and she will pass unscathed through what would have been the accident site.

Some clients opt to continue this type of general information session and book several appointments in a row until all their questions are answered. They return for subsequent readings depending on their need, usually about three to six months apart. Other clients select intuitive life coaching sessions. These are accomplished through specialized readings dedicated to clearing negativity from specific sources. Some examples are: inner children issues, clearing past lives and releasing soul contracts.

Wounded inner children block people from emotional maturity. When traumatic incidents happen during childhood, the child is too immature to process and release the negativity. There are as many inner children as there are retained traumas in one's life. Negative energies from events are absorbed and repressed by the child, resulting in stunted emotional states. Inner children are comprised of ages from conception right up to the client's present age. When past negative emotions are triggered by an event in the present time, the adult displays an immature emotional reaction. Since like attracts like, the inner child that holds similar fear will be the one that is summoned to respond. This is apparent when an adult reacts to an event with a temper tantrum of sorts, similar to how a child would. I have worked with many clients on releasing their inner children, and it can be quite involved. Once inner children are released, the adult responds to similar negative stimuli with a mature attitude and self-control. It's very empowering and entertaining to observe yourself reacting in a totally calm and constructive manner to an event that you previously would have reacted poorly to. Clients tell me that this alone has changed their lives into a more positive and healthy environment for themselves and their families and co-workers.

Unresolved past life events are also incorporated into the ego personality, affecting your life, habits, attitudes, emotions and more. As the negative energy from a past event is released, the corresponding negative personality traits are also absolved. Some examples of these negative traits are: bad habits, anxiety, phobias, anger, depression, jealousy, distrust, racism, physical dis-ease, destructiveness, eating disorders, addictions, and all forms of fear. The reason there are past lives to finish off or release is because the soul was unable to complete this task in a former life. For instance, there could be a relationship that was not fulfilled, or a particular financial situation that you need to learn from still. Everything that was incomplete in a past life is on the "to do" list and will remain there until it is accomplished. The age at which past life events occurred will often resurface when you reach a similar age in this life.

For instance, a lover from a past life or spouse with whom you did not finish or resolve problems with will reappear. You will be attracted to that person again and the liaison will continue until the soul lessons are learned. There are many reasons for incomplete relationships; we are all subject to free will. Often I see that one of the people in the relationship may have been drawn to fight in a war, or may have left their loved one to find work in a faraway town, unable to return.

Lots of clients have past life circumstances that affect them adversely. The angels have helped them to clear this negativity. Common negativity from past lives vary and include being a: musician, soldier, miner, slave, circus performer, animal trainer, lumber jack, prisoner of war, sailor, fisherman, hunter, fortune teller, an opera singer and an actor.

Once these lives are released, the person feels comfortable and can relax, as the fear and habits from the previous lives dissipate. She can move forward into a new way of looking at herself and her surroundings. She attracts more harmonious people and better things into her life; a more peaceful existence is attained.

I am often guided to do an angel healing on clients. This is predominantly to remove as much negativity as possible so that they are able to leap up to their next highest level of joy. This means that had they fallen off their soul path, they can climb back up on it. If they are on their lower or middle soul path, they can jump up to the next higher one. If they are on their highest soul path, they can shoot forward to their next highest level of enlightenment. It also helps them to continue clearings at home more easily, as the momentum of draining negative energy has been jump-started. I find many forms of darkness during an angel healing including blockages in all chakras, dark spots in the aura, dark plugs scattered throughout the body, dark entities, pain bodies, and a whole lot of 'garbage'. I do say garbage because that is literally what

I am shown; garbage being dumped out of the client's body. Sometimes I see a video of a past life, and we remove the stuck negativity from it. Sometimes I am shown trapped inner children and release them. Just about anything can come up during an angel healing. I used to think of them as angel healings at the beginning, but they have grown in strength and power. The Holy Spirit now shows up for the healings and brings with Him all who can help.

The clients relax and focus on their breath. I am guided to clear the body and aura, balance the chakras and get their energy or chi flowing freely again. The energy healing works just as well over the phone as it does in person, because angels have no limitations of time and space. Clients tell me they feel lighter, happier, tingly and comforted. Sometimes they will feel a release of a muscle tension, or relief from a chronic sore back or hip. They also mention that they feel released of burdens.

There are many interesting stories I could tell about readings and what the angels have taught my clients and me. Here are but a few. One client asked a question regarding his daughter who was about to go to court. She had been charged with driving under the influence of alcohol. She had previously been charged with a couple of lesser alcohol-related driving infractions, but had not learned her lesson from them. The angels advised the man that his daughter needed to learn three lessons. They described what aspects she was required to learn for each subject. Firstly, his daughter was an alcoholic and she was to stop drinking alcohol completely and forever. She had no resistance to it, and could not limit herself to one or two drinks on a weekend. Next, she was to learn to be a responsible citizen for the safety of society and herself, especially when behind the wheel of a car. Thirdly, the daughter was required to stop seeing her drinking friends and to cut ties with them. She had tried to stop drinking several times before, but each time, they enticed her to drink with them again. This sent her into a downward spiral of alcoholism. The angels directed my client in methods to help his daughter learn these issues. He was to open the door for her learning, but she had to walk through that door on her own initiative. Her angels said if she declined to learn the lessons, she would be sentenced to incarceration for a time period of three months. If she learned the lessons only part way, she would be sentenced to six weeks of imprisonment. If she changed her life and became a law-abiding citizen and abstained from alcohol, she would then be released of all punishment. If the latter was the case, on the day of the trial she would be led out of the original courtroom and into a different one with a more lenient judge who would liberate her from all charges. The angels advised my client that it was one of his daughter's soul purposes to overcome her alcohol addiction. If she did not overcome it this time, she would be repeatedly 'hit over the head' with increasingly stronger lessons until she cleared herself from her addiction.

I heard from my client shortly after the trial date. He said his daughter had worked very hard and had taken her angels' advice very seriously. He confirmed what the angels had told him; just before her trial time, a court official approached his daughter in the courtroom and directed her to another court room, where the judge fully discharged all offences. To this day, his daughter has completely changed her ways and is leading a sober and law-abiding life. This demonstrates that if someone learns the lesson their soul requires, they don't necessarily need to suffer the consequences of human regulations and procedures. This has been proven in many sessions. Conversely if a person needs to learn a lesson it will be presented to them repeatedly with increasing intensity until the lesson is learned.

Another client began her session asking several questions. After answering her queries her angels were very intent on telling her what was on their minds. They wanted her to know that very soon she would be pregnant; her baby boy would be very healthy, unlike her first child. The woman completely refused to accept that she would become pregnant. She had many reasons to disbelieve. She told me of how it took her over six years of attending fertility clinics, and spending thousands of dollars for her to become pregnant with her first child. She was much older now, and clearly believed herself to be infertile. According to her, it was impossible for her to get pregnant without clinical assistance. Her excited angels were adamant and repeated the information several times, not allowing me to refrain from articulating the tidings of great joy.

About five months later she called for another reading. She told me that she was three months' pregnant. She recounted how she had entirely discounted and then forgotten the communication she had received previously from the angel reading about her upcoming pregnancy. She told me of how she had become ill, and was prescribed medical tests to discover if she was displaying symptoms of an hereditary syndrome that her mother and sister suffered from. First was the blood test. She recounted that she had been totally astounded when her physician advised her of her pregnancy, and immediately remembered her angel's prediction.

She had called this time to ask her angels for confirmation that the baby would be healthy. Because of her age, her doctor had advised her to have amniocenteses, which she feared could possibly cause a spontaneous abortion. After discussing the issue with her angels during the reading, she came to her own realization that even if the baby wasn't healthy, she would not abort. Her angels also reminded her that her boy would be born completely healthy, so if she decided to proceed with the test, the baby would easily withstand the procedure. She still was going to make a final decision over the next few days. The reading released the fear of having the amniocenteses, so she could relax and make a decision with a clear mind. This client called me after her healthy and robust baby boy was born. She said that within a couple of days of having her reading, she decided against having the amniocentesis; she wanted to have her "miracle baby" no matter what the test results showed. The angels will never tell anyone what to do, but they help them to see all sides of their situation and give them information and release fear. This new frame of mind helps people to engage their own intuition and make good and fair decisions.

I have been presented with many clients who feel that they are going to die soon and they are very upset about it. One such client was male, around 50 years of age. He had been experiencing fearful feelings about being in a fatal car accident. His angels agreed with him that he was being warned of an exit that was fast approaching. An exit is what the angels refer to as an option to leave earth life earlier than the final exit of pre-planned death time. Since he was obviously not interested in an early death, he was directed to speak to his angels sincerely and with emphasis. "I choose to remain living on Earth in my healthy body. I refuse to take this exit." Next he was guided to visualize a door leading to the rest of his life. On the door was written: "Jason's door to a happy healthy abundant long life." He was asked to walk through that door and leave behind everything that he did not need anymore. Once this had been accomplished, a huge sense of relief washed over him. His tension was discharged, and his eyes moistened with a few rare tears of joy.

Divine Mother has guided me many times during a reading to put my client on the massage table and do an energy healing. If it is a phone reading, my client is guided to relax and lie down if possible. Angels have no limitations of time or space, so it doesn't matter if the client is right with me or on the other side of the world; the healing is equally effective. I feel Mother's energy flushing through me into the client. This amazing vibrant energy fills the client with everything that is necessary for healing and growth. These healings are constantly increasing in intensity. Sometimes Divine Mother guides me to perform energy healings on groups in my workshops.

Spirit often guides me to lead a client through visualizations for the purpose of clearing, healing, and grounding or for other reasons. The angels create individualized detailed visualizations that are specifically designed for a client's particular needs. Inevitably, the visualizations are perfectly prepared so that the client can visualize them easily because she can relate to them personally. In this way, Spirit can help more intensely. Again, it's the "God helps those who help themselves" idea. The visualization is us helping ourselves; then God and His angels help us to do the rest. The better and stronger the visualization, the better and stronger Spirit can help. I am given a visual of what I am to describe to each client. For example, I will be shown a female client floating in a serene lake totally relaxed, or resting on a beach or sitting near a tree. I usually confirm with her that she likes and feels comfortable with the vision I have just explained to her. Always so far the answer has been similar to: "oh yes, I love floating in water," or "I love sitting on the beach" or "I am so relaxed in my backyard." Then we continue with the visualization which I am guided to express.

One client was incredibly stressed upon arrival for her reading. Divine Mother began the reading. Straight away, I saw the client sitting on a beach and relaxing. I presented this to her and we meditated on it. The rest of the reading went well. When a person is relaxed, her angel guidance flows clearly and quickly through me so I can convey it to her easily. Conversely when someone is anxious, the energy is not as forthcoming; it may be slower and not quite as clear. When the reading was finished she said that the beach was so relaxing and it really helped her. She had recently been having sessions with a therapist who kept telling her to envision herself floating in water while she meditated. She confided to me that she was afraid of water and could hardly swim. She had not been able to relax at all or get into a meditative state while thinking about being in water. She could not focus on the directives of the therapist because she was so uncomfortable with the floating visualization. She was happy to now have this new visualization to work with.

During another reading, the healing came in the form of a magnificent sparkling angel. She was holding a sparkler like the ones I used as a child during fireworks celebrations; the kind that when lit with a match, the sparks come spewing forth. I had not seen this angel before. The angel was golden and sparkling from her halo down to her toes. She was beautiful beyond description. She used the wand as a healing tool, filling my client with her exquisite energy and taught us a visualization for healing that the client could perform at home. After the reading, I asked my client if the visualization was helpful. She said that she absolutely loved sparklers, and that it was the perfect visualization for her. She replied that she could envisage it so well because she enjoyed sparklers and they were her most favourite type of fireworks. She said that she had felt enormous amounts of resplendent energy entering her from the sparkly angel. I found that the better someone can visualize, the better the healing works. The best way to visualize is to find something that you really like and can see really well in your mind's eye.

One of my female clients was very afraid to develop her intuitive abilities. When we explored her past lives, we found that she had secretly been a psychic in a previous existence. She had been exposed by a secret lover whom she had dismissed when she discovered that he was married. He lived in a town nearby, and was afraid she would reveal him as an adulterer. He blew the whistle on her, and she had been hunted, persecuted and finally burned at the stake. In this life, her intuition had been blocked with fear from the past. Now she is happily and eagerly tapping into her clairvoyance.

During another session with a male client, a past life revealed that he had lost his three children to terrible deaths. He admitted that he adamantly refused to be a father in this lifetime. This was destroying his relationship with his wife who desperately wanted children. Once we cleared the past life, his angels guaranteed him that he would not lose any children in this life; that purpose had already been fulfilled. He felt a huge sense of relief; like the weight of the world had been lifted off his shoulders. A gentle smile slowly formed on his lips, as he pondered aloud about how wonderful a dad he could be. I heard from him a couple of years later that he was a proud father of a beautiful little girl, and that he and his wife were awaiting the birth of their second child. They were ecstatic!

A slim male client was cleared of a past life in which he

was detained in a concentration camp. The angels showed me him as a boy about 12 years old catching mice and rats with his hands, and presenting the much prized meat to his starving fellow prisoners. He was a hero to all the other captives, and they fiercely protected him from being detected by the malicious death-camp officers. After hearing me describe the 'video', my client relaxed back in his chair, shook his head and laughed. He told me of a time in this life when he was a boy around 12 years old. For a couple of years, he and his friend frequented an old barn foundation that was fairly close to their homes. There were many mice hiding under the rotting boards and debris around the derelict foundation. He caught mice with his bare hands and placed them into a box that his friend was holding. He swiftly caught numerous mice easily with his agile body, and a radar-like sense, that pinpointed the position of each mouse. The boys would keep the mice for a short time, and then let them go. My client said catching mice made him feel valuable and happy. The funny part of the story is that one day he was bitten on his hand by a mouse. His mom took him to the doctor where she told the doctor of her son's habit of catching mice. After examining the bite, the doctor said, "This bite looks pretty serious; you may have to measure him up for a pine box." After that, my client stopped catching mice; instead he and his friend captured frogs. Frogs have no teeth!

I read for a female client who had a past life as a house slave. There was no escape for her. She was severely over worked with household chores and her duties of taking care of the spoiled children. According to her 'owners', she could never do anything well enough, and was always admonished for everything she did. She had no opportunity to voice her opinion, and had no prospect of generating a better existence for herself. Into this present life, she brought with her the previous life's low self-esteem and minimal self-respect. Her inability to make decisions and stand up for herself along with feeling that she couldn't do anything right, made her life intolerable. She hated to do household chores and couldn't stand spoiled children. When she ultimately understood that these unwanted feelings originated from a past existence, she felt as if the sun was shining on her for the first time in her life. Understanding is a pivotal point for my clients. That's when their lives start to change and grow in new and wonderful directions.

Soul contracts are decided upon before the Earth journey and are an agreement between two or more souls. Negative soul contracts are designed to finish off negative energy between the individuals from previous lives. These types of soul contracts include negative relationships between a boss and employee, husband and wife, parent and child, and owner and pet. They include negative energy between neighbours, co-workers, friends and relatives and also opposing groups of people. There is an obvious distinct difference in behavioural patterns between the two parties that are not tolerated by each other. Distrust and non-understanding of the other's ways, habits, beliefs, opinions, ideals and views give rise to non-acceptance and disharmony.

When one of the people in a two-person relationship develops unconditional love for the other, the contract is broken. The intention is to completely be released and set free, creating forward motion on the spiritual path. A woman for example who is able to perform this duty is highly regarded in her soul group. When a major soul contract is finished, the result may be a divorce, or quitting an important job. This will result in a huge release for her physically and emotionally. She may have become very tired or even ill due to the large contract hanging over her head. The contract can feel very heavy, as if wearing lead boots, restraining her from moving forward on her life path and spiritual journey.

The significance of soul contracts extend beyond the two people and into their soul groups. When a soul contract is finished there is a big celebration on the other side, because it is the end of an important phase of that person's life. There is the closing of the old door and the opening of a new one. This represents a new direction in life; a new era. The person's whole soul group is raised into a higher vibration.

Sometimes I am guided to take note of a particular visualization as I am to teach it to others individually during readings or in workshops, as it is helpful for many people. They are visualizations that are to be done in a meditative state. These are tools that can be used to augment clearing, healing, and grounding which in turn aid other important issues. One of these I call the Mother Earth Meditation. It was presented to me during a reading, and I was told to make a special note of it, as I was to teach it to as many people as possible and therefore, is included in the exercises below. I use and teach this guided meditation more often than all the others put together. This visualization cleanses negativity that is ready to be released. It is a grounding exercise that expands focus, relaxation and peacefulness. It is also a healing method that replaces negative energy with positive love energy. Moreover, it is colour therapy. Every colour has its own vibratory properties that heal similar misaligned vibrations in your body. This promotes balance and good energy flow in your being. Whatever colour you envision is the right colour to use at that time. When doing this meditation, if no colour presents itself to me, I use my favourite colour which is green. Green attracts me because I require its healing properties more than any other colour. Furthermore, this meditation brings you in line with Mother Earth's vibration, and keeps you progressing with her as she transforms herself on her journey to ascension. It ensures that your energy is aligned with the Universe, and keeps you learning everything you need to know for your soul purpose path. When you are out of sorts or unhappy, it is because you are not in line with your soul purpose. Practicing this meditation grounds you to Mother Earth. I was shown this meditation/visualization as I was becoming aware of Mother Earth's energy changing from third dimension through to fifth and beyond. This is a progressive movement of Earth that brings love and light to herself and her inhabitants. All those who are on board are able to incorporate life's challenges much more easily than those who are not. When I feel any less than fully peaceful and loving, I do this meditation. I feel the peace and joy returning to me. My clients tell me that this visualization has helped them immensely and especially during times of crisis.

It is important to understand what the different dimensions are and how Earth is changing. The third dimension is characterized by those who only believe in what they see and feel physically such as a car or chair. They are unaware of, and not accepting that there is spiritual activity in their being, on Earth and in the Universe. Fourth dimensional people are aware of spiritual activity in their lives and around them. For instance they feel a presence of Universal energy or at least know that there is some sort of Higher Power. Perhaps they believe in the Universe, God, Great Spirit, and Divine Beings, such as Guardian Angels or Spirit Guides. They are aware that they receive some sort of intuition, perhaps through gut feelings, synchronicities or dreams guiding them through lives. Fifth dimension is a step beyond the latter and is the entrance to living in Heaven on Earth. It is a place of peace, love and joy and all good things. It is characterized as consistently being on an even keel emotionally, no matter what is happening in one's surroundings. It is surrendering to oneness with Creator, generating incredible bliss.

Many times during a reading I have been guided to cut negative cords between my client and a person with whom 'he' had a relationship. Cutting of cords is important as it releases destructive aspects of a past or present relationship, but always leaves positive or love ties in place. The method of the cutting of negative cords is included in the exercises below. One of my clients was having a lot of difficulty in releasing himself from his ex-wife. He was divorced for over 20 years, and had been in his second marriage for 12 years. Time is irrelevant where negative cords are concerned. They are just as potent 20 years later as they are at the time of origin. The angels guided me through a visualization which I narrated to him, as the client's effort and intention is always the biggest part of the healing process. I have been asked to do this visualization with many clients since then. Inevitably, the clients tell me afterwards how much relieved and lighter they feel after cutting the cords. Often they are able to transform the negative relationship into a much kinder and mutually helpful one. Sometimes the person we cut cords with has passed away. This allows the client to redefine the past relationship, instilling peace, empathy and closure. This is especially helpful for clients who have lost a loved one before they have developed mutual respect and understanding or been able to create a harmonious liaison.

Many times clients have been abused by an alive or

passed person, and cutting the cords releases much of the despair encircling such damaging encounters. Negative cords come from relationships, acquaintances and anytime when negative energy is created through thoughts words or actions. This can be between two or more people. Negative cords hold people down; similar to ropes that secure a boat to a dock. It's difficult to jettison forward while tethered. Some people think of themselves as being involved in a relationship in which they are trapped, stuck, disrespected, suffocated or locked down by a ball and chain. These relationships, present or past, include those with partners, lovers, parents, children, siblings, bosses, and anyone who stirs negative emotions within. I see the cords in my mind's eye as black ropes of similar size and shape that tie boats to a dock in the harbour. They can be as thick as the ropes used to tether ocean liners, or as thin as the type that fasten watercraft to the dock, or any size in between. Once the cords are cut, there is a feeling of enormous relief for the client. The person who was at the other end of the cord also feels the release of past baggage on some level. Whether the two people involved decide to continue their relationship or end it, they will have a more pleasant association, should they have future encounters. Positive love cords always remain in place and are the foundation for a new connection with the same person and also for creating future compassionate affiliations for new and old relationships. It's much quicker and easier to create promising connections with people once old fears have been removed. Archangel Michael is always called in to cut the cords, and each time he is eager to be of assistance.

After cutting the cords, I am directed to lead my clients in a visualization that creates a protective shield around the outside of their aura. This deflects any incoming negative energy so it is not absorbed into their energy field. Negativity can be absorbed from many places and people, so it is necessary to protect yourself against it. I am led to tell my clients to repeat this exercise regularly, sometimes daily or once a week. This ensures that the protective energy is replenished and remains strong. It is important to end the exercise with envisioning the other person sending an arrow with a negative cord attached to it, and the protective shell repelling the arrow. This greatly reinforces the shield and generates an even stronger protective fortress around you. Sending the arrow back to the person doesn't hurt him; it is his own energy. Sending back energy actually helps the person because he will eventually understand on a sub-level that the projection of negativity is redundant. It is not being effective in any way as it is not being anchored anywhere. Ultimately he will stop shooting negativity in your direction and hopefully to others as well. I have also been advised that by reflecting negative energy back to the person, it causes the "negative x negative = positive" (algebra) effect which releases negative karma for him. You are actually helping this person on his spiritual journey by performing this task. It can only help you simultaneously. This will gradually cause him to change to a more positive attitude. Note that positive love energy is absorbed through the protective layer.

EXERCISES

The exercises in this book are primarily meant for the reader who is truly on, or who wants to be on the spiritual path. Trust that you were guided to this book particularly to learn from the exercises. When the angels portrayed to me the concept of this book, they expressed their great enthusiasm predominantly for the exercise portion of the book. They channelled these exercises to me with the intention that many people would advance on their spiritual journey through their efforts. The exercises are designed to help you gain illumination. Reading them alone will help you to raise your vibration. Doing the exercises will demonstrate to the Universe that you are doing your part, and that you are ready for input and advancement from your angels and Higher Power. They will help you to discover your life purpose, guide you forward toward your next level of enlightenment, and help to generate love, peace and joy into your life.

Focused Breath

There are three parts to a focused breath. <u>This breath is used at the beginning of all meditations and visualizations.</u> It calms the mind and prepares your body for deep physical relaxation which is necessary for successful sessions.

Close your eyes, palms up in your lap; sit tall with a straight spine. Relax into this position.

Belly: Place one hand on your belly, over your belly button. Breathe in deeply while you see and feel your hand rising and falling with your breath. The belly is filled first, at the beginning of each breath. Try this for a few breaths. Exhale gently and relax.

Ribs: Place your other hand on your ribs at the side of your body. Start by filling the belly, then feel your hand move outward as your breath inflates your ribs. Practice these two parts of the breath a few times.

Chest: Place a hand on your upper chest just below your collar bone. Fill your belly, ribs, and finally your chest. Feel your hand rising as your lungs fill up with the third part of the breath.

Release breath fully. Don't push the air out, but simply relax as it leaves your lungs. Be sure to keep your posture with a straight spine, and don't collapse your lungs as the air is released. Practice all three parts of the breath a few times; to be sure you remember it.

Focus on your breath as the air passes through your nostrils and down deep into your belly, ribs and chest. Focus on the air leaving your body and again passing through your nostrils. If you have a thought that distracts you from focusing on your breath, gently pluck it from your mind and return your attention to your breath. Often during our daily lives breathing is shallow and ineffective. Breathing deeply allows Life Force to enter your body bringing good energy, healing, clarity, health and peace.

Mother Earth Meditation/Visualization

It may help you to do the visualization better if you first try it outside with your feet on the ground or in the grass. However, whether you are on the 40th floor of a building or deep down in a cave, it will work. Visualization creates changes within. Your part is the visualization and Spirit's part is to help you. The better you can visualize the more effective it will be. When I first started visualizing I had great difficulty seeing colours and objects. I practiced a lot and gradually became much better at it. Just do your best, no more and no less.

Negativity surfaces in layers much as an onion has many layers. When you release the outer skin, the next layer is exposed and becomes ready for removal. Clearing and releasing meditations must therefore be done on a regular basis, and especially when you are feeling incomplete, out of sorts or unhappy. I do this exercise morning and night and implement additional times during the day as needed.

Start with a few Focused Breaths in your best meditation pose: lying down or sitting up. Count down slowly from 10 to 1, deeply relaxing into a peaceful state. As you count down, you can envision yourself going down in an elevator, an escalator or stairs, or whatever you feel most comfortable with. Have the intention of doing the Mother Earth Meditation and ask your angels for help. If a specific colour comes to your mind, trust that it is the best healing colour for your bodily needs at that time. Otherwise, visualize green, because it exudes peacefulness. Black is not a colour; it is the absence of light and cannot be used to bring light in.

Envision yourself in the middle of a dark cloud which represents all negativity that is ready for release.

Visualize the beautiful energy of your preferred colour underneath your feet. See it swirling in the earth, building energy and becoming more powerful and vigorous. Know that this is supreme energy for clearing, healing and grounding. Feel the unconditional love, caring, kindness and provision that Mother Earth feeds you.

See the earth colour slowly rise up your left foot, up to your knee, thrusting the negative cloud ahead of it. The earth colour then comes up to your left hip, up the left side of your torso, up the left side of your neck, driving the dark cloud ahead of it. The Mother Earth colour then goes up the left side of your head, and does a 180 degree turn over the top of your head. It starts to come down the right side of your head, down the right side of your neck, still pushing the dark cloud of negativity ahead. The Mother Earth supreme colour energy now comes down the right side of your torso, to your right hip, to your right leg and finally out your right foot. Always envision the dark cloud being pushed ahead of the swirling earth colour.

After the cloud has been removed from your right foot, keep thrusting the negative cloud ever deeper into Mother Earth and finally down to her molten lava where she dissolves it easily. Mother Earth is grateful to have negative energy sent to her as it enables her to cleanse herself. Negativity that is sent to her multiplies with the negative within her, and then is released as substantial positive energy. This is also how the release of negative karma works.

Continue circulating the Mother Earth colour from the swirling energy ball under your feet, up your left side and over the top of your head and down the right side, back into the energy ball. Feel it continuously swirling throughout your whole body consistently increasing in intensity. Sense the beautiful energy cleansing and healing you. Breathe this impeccable healing colour into your lungs, and revel in the exquisite energy it brings to your whole self. See the colour filling every cubic inch of you.

Next expand this peaceful energy to the outside of your aura, filling your whole being with lovely joyful energy. You are now in a bubble of perfect healing energy designed for your specific needs.

Once you feel the energy strongly, visualize roots as in tree roots growing downward from the bottom of your feet, spreading and extending deep down into the earth, grounding you to Mother Earth. Feel the connection to her and the strength and love that she brings you. Enjoy this incredible sensation for a while.

Cutting Negative Cords

Do a few Focused Breaths in the best meditation pose for you, lying down or sitting.

Say aloud: "Archangel Michael, please cut the negative cords between me and (name of person with whom you have had a negative exchange or relationship with.)"Visualize yourself in your aura and see the other person, for example a man, in his aura in front of you. Now see or imagine all the negative cords between you and him. Envision Archangel Michael cutting the cords with his light sabre. He slashes all the cords easily from all around the outside of your aura. Watch as all the cords fall to the ground and disintegrate. Ashes left from the cords are swept up and taken away by the angels. Larger cords are caused by relationships that have been very challenging or destructive. In these cases, plugs similar to electrical wall plugs connect the cords to the two bodies. See Michael pull these plugs out of you and give them to an angel for safe disposal. Michael then fills each and every extraction site where the plugs were removed with his intense healing energy.

Breathe for the void.

Say out loud: "Michael please fill me with your light energy." Now see Michael put his hand on you, usually at the top of your head, or your upper chest just under your neck and fill you with his beautiful bluish-purplish healing light. Allow it to fill you and your aura up completely. Breathe it into your lungs and visualize his healing energy filling every cubic millimeter of your whole being including your aura. Often his friend, I call her the Pink Angel or Archangel Ariel, comes with him. She fills you with pink healing love light. See yourself being filled with beautiful pink energy, and revel in the loving affection that she endows upon you.

Protection

Once you have cleared yourself of negativity, it is important to protect yourself against further negative attachments. Guardian Angels are responsible for personal protection. The aura is your energy field and is about three-to four-feet outside of your body, and resembles an egg shape if you are standing. Sometimes I am shown an eggshell-type material, and often a shiny titanium covering. There are other specific protective materials available, depending on what type of protection a person requires. Your Guardian Angel will know with what material to make your protective shell.

Visualize yourself with your aura around you and ask your Guardian Angel to place a protective "eggshell" around the outside of your aura that is perfect for the protection you will need for the day/week/weeks. Remember the better you visualize this, the more powerful the result.

Next, visualize a generic person sending you a negative cord with an arrow on the front of it. The arrow hits your protective layer and reflects back to that person, leaving your protective layer perfectly intact and keeping you completely safe from all negativity.

Always thank your angels whenever they do something nice for you. They appreciate gratitude and sing a song and perform a dance of joy that inspires to the very soul. They are humble and bountiful and work hard for us so we will succeed, even when we are oblivious to their support.

CHAPTER 11

CHANNELLING

My life has been a series of episodes that I haven't had clarity about till much later. Only then am I privy to the information that allows me to see the whole picture, or at least as much of the picture as my perception can understand. When I get strong intuition, I am asked to sit down and listen, and sometimes to get a paper and start writing. The following is case in hand, as my angels ask me to trust that the channelling coming in is important and needs to be recorded and shared in my book.

I have been guided to visit my mom's cottage on Georgian Bay to write my book. It is a beautifully sunny day, the first one this spring that I have been able to enjoy so fully. The wind is very strong and the waves are crashing in along the sand beach. The whitecaps are so numerous and for the first time I can remember, the waves are rolling in with one humongous roar, as opposed to hearing each successive one following the last. The water is such a beautiful deep Mediterranean blue; the hue that is only apparent in very deep water. Closer to shore, the greens and bluey-greens are perceptible and gorgeous. I have always been drawn to water for the vast spiritual energy it provides. I close my eyes and the channelling begins...

Spirit says:

"I take this time out of my busy schedule to tell you that I am looking for the ones who will be following me and their

hearts to heaven. I mean heaven on earth, and all those who choose to come are welcome. The ascension has begun. It is time now to prepare yourselves for this event. First you must release all or as many negative thoughts and habits from your daily routine, and your lives as possible. These are the steps for accomplishing this:

When you think a negative thought, visually pluck it from your head and release it to your Guardian Angel for safe deposit. Replace it with a positive thought related to the same issue. There is always a positive side even though it may be difficult for you to see it at the time. Gradually you will be able to recognize these negative thoughts as they are emerging, and you will be able to stop them earlier and earlier until they disappear. This will take some time, so get started immediately. This includes negative thoughts about people, animals, Earth, trees and plants, climate, jobs, and lifestyle and so on. Also be aware of all negative traps such as jealousy, hate, racism, anger, greed, destruction and all negativity. Basically, all fear needs to be released. Fear is anything negative. Therefore, you will be releasing fear and replacing it with love. Love is everything positive. Examples of love: compassion, caring, helping, joy, laughter, smiling, abundance, welcoming, kindness, giving and bliss.

It will help for you to write a manifestation list where you will see it regularly throughout the day to remind you. Add this to it: 'I am so happy and grateful now that I have always and only positive thoughts words and actions.'

You must bring into yourself as much light as possible, that is, as much as you can possibly absorb, and then continue bringing it in always. The way to do this is to visualize yourself with a 'cord of light' connected to your soul at your solar plexus and extending to Universal Light Source. This cord constantly brings in a flow of light, filling your being with Source light which feeds your soul and spirit with love from your Higher Power. Light Source is always available to anyone who asks for it. It helps you to connect more deeply with your inner being or soul, and your Higher Self. It gives you light energy so you can move more quickly up the ladder of enlightenment. It helps you to find your soul purpose for this lifetime, and all else that is important for your growth.

Visualizing is very important as in the scriptures: 'God helps those who help themselves.' Visualizing is your part, so the better you can visualize, the better the result you will receive. Your Higher Power and angels will give you Divine help. Much practice may be necessary before you can visualize well, so don't stress over it, do the best you can, no more and no less.

You must allow yourself the freedom to seek and find all abundance, especially spiritual abundance. Spiritual abundance means to be wide awake consciously and to see and feel all goodness and light in the world. There are steps to this. You must love yourself and all others unconditionally. All others means All There Is, including all people, animals and all aspects of Mother Earth and everything else that exists. Be compassionate to those who are less fortunate than you are spiritually, financially, mentally, physically and emotionally. Be understanding to others. Live your life in a humble way, knowing that you are also a work in progress.

Release all judgment. The person you are judging could easily have been you; 'But for the grace of God go I'. To judge others is to assume a role that you are not capable of. Know that you cannot possibly see the 'whole picture', and therefore cannot possibly make any correct judgment of any sort. If you understand that everyone is doing the best they can with what they have, then you have more compassion and understanding toward them. Accepting others for who they are does not mean that you condone what they have done, rather that you accept that they have done what they have done. This allows you to move forward.

The main important issue to discuss is the fourth dimension, and how to attain it. There are many paths that lead to Oneness. All paths are effective, although some will take longer than others. It is of no consequence which path you choose, it is the final result that is the only consideration. To be in the fourth dimension is to live your life every minute and every second in a state of love. Love for yourself, love for God/Spirit, love for all mankind, love for all animals and for Mother Earth, and the Universe. This is created by being mindful. It is accomplished by living in the moment as much as possible and also, by keeping your mind on love and/or God. Give yourself reminders, such as writing an 'L' for love on your hand or where you will see it often. As you do your work during the day, you will find that your mind needs to concentrate on your task. This is necessary in your world. It is only possible for the human mind to focus well on one thing at a time. Be forgiving of yourself. During the times when you can focus on love, do it and do it as often as possible.

During the transition of Earth into the final phases of the fourth and fifth dimensions, there are many grave changes, not only to the Earth's surface, but deep beneath the crust, in the middle layers of the earth. It is similar to a ball having been injected with hydrogen peroxide. The Earth's vibration is bubbling up to the surface and affecting all who live there. This vibration is the marked access of all Earth's inhabitants to 'pack their suitcases' if they are coming to the fifth dimension.

The fifth dimension is comprised of the love from the fourth dimension melding with the attributes of the fifth, which we will now discuss. The fifth dimension is comprised of love, joy, peace, clarity, compassion, and all abundance which leads to living in bliss. Bliss is the all-encompassing vibratory sensation of living in the highest form of enlightenment available to mankind on Earth at this time. There will come a time when the sixth and seventh and many more dimensions are also available, this will happen in the foreseeable future. So, how do you get to the fifth? Once you have attained the fourth, the fifth will naturally be available to you, and you will attain it much more readily and easily than the fourth. It is a natural progression of Light Force, which will carry you along as a stream carries a leaf. But let's not get ahead of ourselves."

At this point I was asked to write newsletters, facilitate workshops and start writing chapters for this book. I had already begun to do workshops in my home. I wanted to help people learn the same skills I had developed; to help them navigate their path without falling into the pitfalls that had slowed me down so much. I think that if I had received more help with my journey, I could have accomplished the same amount of growth in less than one-third of the time. In these workshops I taught attendees about recognizing and increasing intuition, getting in touch with their guardian angel, seeing auras, feeling earth energies, removing negativity, absorbing light, and a host of other spiritual activities. Spirit was asking me to provide more workshops that would help to prepare people to unite with Him. I was eager to help in any way I could, so I began.

BOOK TWO

COMPANION WORKBOOK

Channelling from Spirit:

"Now is the time for all my children to come to me. I am waiting patiently, but urge you to come forth quickly. Many people do not heed my warnings, but you who are reading this book know of what I say. You are the ones who are feeling your intuition and who are ready and willing to move forward on your Spiritual Journey and Soul Purpose. You are the ones who cause me the greatest of joy, and I shower you with love. I send my angels to help each of you learn what is necessary to become one with me and consciously remember my kingdom. The most important thing you need to know, and which will always lead you in the highest direction, is that you must do everything in a state of love. Do this and you shall succeed

INTRODUCTION

I was asked by Spirit to reiterate how I had navigated my journey, and cleared my soul path, so others could gain knowledge from my experience. This would demonstrate techniques and develop ways for them to follow their own path. The following chapters are a description of what transpired from Spirit's direction.

I was instructed to create "On Wings of Love" newsletters and facilitate workshops once a month. I was given a channelled message to transcribe for each newsletter, and was guided to expand and explain the channelling through the remainder of the newsletter. During my "On Wings of Love" workshops I was led to clarify the newsletter further, include examples and develop experiential exercises for enriched spiritual understanding and growth. The members of my workshop were to be the "test group" for me to gauge how well the exercises worked and to build my confidence in the channelled exercise program. Following each workshop I was to record the activities as a chapter for my future book so that people world-wide could be included in the angel's plan to raise the spiritual awareness and vibration of the planet and all of humanity. For further reading, there are more newsletters and blog posts on my website.

Book Two can be thought of as a text-book for educational purposes. Similar to a mathematics text, the explanation comes first, and then the exercises follow. As in math, if you do the exercises, you gain more advancement and learn more completely, than if you just read them.

After I finished the chapters which became Book Two,

I was guided to write my life-history which became Book One. The angels thought that it was important for readers to connect with me and through gaining trust and understanding, be inspired to grow spiritually themselves. Comprehending that the exercises are what boosted me forward on my spiritual journey, the readers were to realize that they too now have the tools to increase their vibration, intuition and enlightenment.

CHAPTER 12

INTUITION AND MEDITATION

Intuition and Trust

One of the first things I learned was to trust the intuition I was receiving. I learned that if I trusted it, and acted on it I would be rewarded by receiving more. When I ignored or second-guessed my intuitive feelings I would be void of intuitive messages for a while. I read as many books as were assigned to me by my guiding forces. One book that had many significant meanings and values for me was "*Journey to Self-Realization*" by Parmahansa Yogananda. He wrote: "Intuition is soul guidance appearing naturally in man in those instances when his mind is calm." I found this quote particularly helpful in explaining why, when I was not in a calm mood, my intuition was lacking. Also I would obtain false information especially if I had an emotional attachment to the outcome of the question I was asking. It was so wonderful to be reading books written by people who had intuition. It made me feel more normal! I absorbed as much as I could. Spiritual books coupled with teachings from the angels helped me to develop methods that proved helpful.

To avoid my emotions from interfering with receiving clear messages, I developed a technique whereby I pretended to be a 'fly on the wall,' watching myself ask the questions. By becoming the observer I was able to distance my emotions from the process of asking and receiving. It worked really well and I became quite adept at separating myself from my emotions. The best way for me to tune into a state of calmness was through meditation.

Meditation

Meditation can be utilized in many ways. Often people when running or walking or doing any kind of sport enter a meditation-mindfulness mode, perhaps without even recognizing it as such. Mindfulness is a state of mind where you stop thinking about the future and the past, and are completely absorbed in the moment. That is when your mind relaxes and your inner being or soul emerges. Meditation is a process of deep relaxation where the mind becomes rejuvenated, helping you to feel well-rested and in harmony with self and all things around you. During the day, the mind is very active with many thoughts. During sleep, the subconscious mind is active in dreams. During some types of meditation, the mind is inactive, often called no-mind and therefore restful and peaceful.

Meditation is different for everyone, and there are many ways and means by which people use meditation. If you count the number of different types of meditations you may find that there are hundreds or even thousands of ways to meditate. Finding the best one for you will be presented to you if you only ask your guides. There are many benefits you will receive from meditation and I have included some of the ones that I have found most helpful.

For many it is a time when one sits quietly while focusing on Divine or Universal energies. This can be accomplished by using the Focused Breath and releasing unwanted thoughts. This will keep your mind clear. Focusing on the breath brings you into the present moment and therefore into the place of soul-awareness. Meditation increases focus and concentration, which helps generally in life and work. It opens channels of intuitive energy that flow into you, giving you feelings of peace, love, joy, light and all positive and good things. Meditation is helpful on all levels; physically, mentally, emotionally and spiritually.

Physically, meditation increases a feeling of well-being. If you are very tired and feel like you need a long nap, but are unable to take the time, you can use meditation to energize you. By breathing life force or prana into your lungs and absorbing it into your body, in a relatively short time you will feel energized and ready to continue your day. It can be used to focus on areas of the body that are in pain, thus reducing the unpleasant sensation. Many people have told me that they use meditation to reduce their pain to the extent that they no longer need pain medication.

Mentally, meditation is used to relax the mind. We are often run by the many thoughts going through our minds. We multi-task and are constantly on the go, neglect to breathe deeply and have difficulty relaxing during the day. Sometimes the mind is still churning at night and it is a challenge to turn it off to get a good restful night's sleep. Meditation calms the mind and for most people it is the only time the mind is restful.

Emotionally, meditation puts everything into a calm perspective. By being in the present moment, one can release fear of future and regret of the past. It brings increasing amounts of serenity. Many people tell me that once they start meditating they are able to be weaned off of anti-depressants and other medications as their feelings of depression and anxiety decrease and their feelings of joy and happiness increase.

Spiritually, meditation is the doorway to intuition. It inspires you to attain a greater understanding of your life and increases ability to deal with all circumstances. It opens the heart, increasing love; decreasing fear and helping you make good decisions. It brings you closer to Creator which enhances all aspects of your life immensely.

Grounding meditations are very effective to restore the natural feeling of connection to Mother Earth and help you to get back to nature. Grounding increases focus, concentration, peacefulness, relaxation and your state of well-being, increasing your feelings of belonging on Earth. Grounding is incorporated in the Mother Earth Meditation where roots are visualized coming out the feet and into the earth.

Meditation is the only way I have found so far to connect with the Universe in a profoundly deep way. Intuition includes the ability to tune in to all the vast unending knowledge of the Universe which will help you in your life choices and beyond. During meditation, while the mind is at rest, information from the Universe is allowed to bypass the scrutinizing ego-mind, and come directly through the soul. This creates the channel which enables intelligence to be brought into the daily lives of those who are willing to listen. This is your direct connection to your Higher Power. Without this connection, life often seems pointless, empty and as if something is missing. Once you have the ability to communicate with your Higher Power, life becomes fuller, more understandable and meaningful. You will find that everything has a purpose and significance, and that there are extremely few if any chance meetings, or coincidences. Receiving intuition is very profound.

It's really very simple; the soul receives Divine or Holy Spirit energy which is intuition or soul guidance. The soul is the part of every being that is the individual spark or piece of the Creator/Spirit. The Intuitive Process starts with calmness. When my mind was busy at work, or talking or thinking, I had no detectable intuitive thoughts or energy emerging. In the beginning, it was only in the relaxed state of quietness, often through meditation, that I could hear or feel messages. The angels helped me to develop grounding exercises that helped me focus, relax and bring a feeling of well-being to myself. Clearing practices were introduced to me by the angels that I adopted gratefully. Protecting my self from interference of static and unwanted energies was essential. A friend of mine taught me a meditation which is called "Stillness Within." This helped me to gain one-pointed focus that was crucial for me to achieve deeper tranquillity. This allowed my mind to relax even more, so the intuitive ideas could be deciphered better. The Stillness Within meditation brought me to a place of heightened awareness which is where I needed to be in order to hear the delicate energies of the angels. There are several additional steps that are important in order to receive intuition and will be discussed in depth in the following chapters. I agree with Parmahansa Yogananda when he said: "Attune yourself to the active inner guidance; the Divine voice has the answer to every dilemma of life."

EXERCISE

Stillness Within is one of the first meditations I learned and one that I still use today, especially when I am having trouble focusing. Many people have told me that they have had much success with this meditation, and that they can get deeper with it than with other meditations they have tried.

Stillness Within Meditation

Start by taking four to five Focused Breaths. On your next breath, exhale very slowly and envision your breath as a ribbon or stream of white light emerging from you and travelling farther and farther away. Keep adding breaths of white light to the ribbon so it is a continuous stream of white light going on forever. Continue to add breaths to the ribbon as it keeps going on… and on… and on… forever into eternity. Continue for five to ten minutes or until you are completely focused on the ribbon of light and in a full state of peace.

Now gently and slowly remaining deep in the meditation, bring your focus inward, away from the ribbon and bring your attention to your inner being…your soul. Experience and feel the *absolute stillness* within. Sometimes I feel the stillness in my head, and sometimes in my heart and solar plexus area, either location works. Breathe into the stillness for about 10 minutes or longer. This meditation creates unequivocal peace and a potent conscious connection to your soul and Higher Power.

CHAPTER 13

POSITIVE THINKING

The angels advised me to write this newsletter because positive thinking is one of the most important aspects for advancement of mind, body and soul.

Excerpt from my *On Wings of Love* Newsletter "*Positive Thinking*", May, 2012

"Whether you think you can, or think you can't, you're right." Henry Ford

"Positive thinking has largely been ignored for generations. It is time now to put an end to negative thinking and to realize that what you sow is what you reap. This means that positive thoughts you put out to the Universe will be reflected back to you: this is what you are manifesting into your life as per the Universal Law of Attraction. When someone puts emotion into a thought, the Universe reacts by sending that person more of what they sent out. This happens equally for positive and negative thoughts. Realizing this gives insight as to how important your thoughts are...they are shaping your future. When you get angry and fill yourself with negative emotion, you are creating more of that for your future. When you are happy and filled with love and joy and all positive thoughts, you are creating more of that for your future. Which one do you want?

The ultimate goals of Positive Thinking are firstly to

cease the accumulation of Negative Karma that will only return to you to be released at some later date, and secondly, to attract to yourself good and positive things and events, so you can have a happy, kind and loving life.

Much of society gives us negative input, sometimes from family members, friends and acquaintances, often from learning institutions and most certainly from newspapers and newscasts. It takes courage and a strong sense of intention to be free of negativity in order to rise above the general public. It is necessary to become conscious of negativity surrounding you. It is important to surround yourself as much as possible with positive thinking people. Negative people can often drag you down to their level, leaving you down in the dumps and feeling drained. However, as you develop more positive thoughts, words and actions, people around you will become more positive through "osmosis" and you will find it becomes easier to be around them.

The challenge is to recognize negativity in yourself and others. Recognition is the key to change. Once aware of it, you can take the necessary steps to remove negativity from your life. Be aware of negativity in actions and words of yourself and others. As you recognize negative words or actions in yourself, you will start to catch them earlier, and soon you will recognize and stop negative thoughts as they are formulating in your mind. Gradually negative thoughts will cease altogether. Then you will have always and only positive thoughts, words and actions.

If something negative that you have to deal with is approaching, look at it from a neutral or the 'fly on the wall' perspective. This helps to dissolve negativity. Having reduced the fear, the problem won't look as foreboding, and a solution will be easier to find.

Know that when seen through the 'big picture', there is a positive reason behind every challenging event in life. Often the reason is to release Negative Karma. This release lightens the load and reduces the baggage, creating a more happy and peaceful life.

Living a life of positivity is highly important. Remember the Universal Law of Attraction will bring in more of what you are radiating out. Always be mindful of your energy output! The energy you put out today creates your future."

One of the first advantageous things I learned was positive thinking. The angels told me that by changing my thinking patterns it actually changed the pathways in my mind into new positive thinking for the long-term. Subsequent information would be automatically processed in a positive way. This was very intriguing; I would have long-term effects for something that I had previously thought would only last a few minutes. Suddenly the prospect of positive thinking and the work it would involve seemed much more worthwhile. Several years later, I learned of the scientific discovery that neuropathways in the brain are actually changed as thinking changes. New pathways are formed and old unused pathways fade away. This proved scientifically what the angels had told me years before, and admittedly it was somewhat gratifying to see scientists proving angel knowledge. I set my mind to be aware of all negative thoughts and pluck them out, replacing them with positive or opposite thoughts. I decided to make it a habit.

The best and most helpful thing I did was to *manifest* my desire to think positively. There are many examples I could tell about how positive thinking has changed my life. The exercise that had the most impact was when I added to my manifestation list: "I am so happy and grateful now that I have always and only positive thoughts." This affirmation alone changed my life. I wrote more items on my list and put it in a place where I would see it often. I read it with emphasis at least twice a day. I went from having many negative thoughts to having virtually none in a matter of two weeks. For the first few days, I had full negative thoughts before I recognized them as such. This quickly progressed to me noticing a negative thought while it was half-way developed, then a quarter of the way, and very soon to just before the thought was conceived. Then the negative thoughts ceased completely. After a few weeks I changed my manifestation list, and since I had conquered my negative thoughts, neglected to include that sentence on my new list. After a couple of weeks, I noticed that I was having negative thoughts again. I quickly squished in: "I have always and only positive thoughts" to the top of the list and soon the undesirable notions receded. Shortly thereafter, I changed it to: "I have always and only positive thoughts, words and actions." I now automatically include this most important and helpful concept on each and every manifestation list I make.

Another important way of releasing negative thoughts and replacing them with positive thinking was the "Grab and Toss" method the angels taught me. I found this progressively helpful in my new quest for constructive thinking. It is described in an exercise below.

I made an intention to follow all the directives of the above channelling verbatim. The subconscious mind takes in and remembers everything it sees, hears, feels, tastes and smells. I made a strong intention to rise above the confines of our negative society, and became conscious of negativity surrounding me, and noticed where it was coming from. I did my best to avail myself more to those who had a positive outlook and to avoid the negative people. Negative friends and acquaintances with whom I had socialized surprisingly stopped calling or moved away. I reduced the time I spent reading newspapers and watching newscasts and began looking for inspirational stories and motivating accounts in books and magazines.

For encounters in life that I anticipated might have a negative duration or outcome, I learned to project the situation to my Higher Power. I visualized the person or people involved and surrendered the situation to the Universe with the intention of creating the best possible outcome for all. I sent love into the setting ahead of time. Having reduced the fear in me by giving control to my higher authority, inevitably, when the meeting arrived, it would turn out to be a productive and helpful gathering with a higher purpose than could have been foreseen.

I knew that when seen through the big picture, there was a positive reason behind every challenging event in life. I started to look for the often so obvious message or lesson that each negative event offered. Frequently the reasons for the event were more comprehensible when reviewing the situation afterward and especially from an unemotional state.

At the beginning of my spiritual awareness and growth I was a young mother. I would find myself irritated sometimes with the normal noise and antics of my children particularly when I was stressed from other challenges in my life. I would calm myself and suppress my irritation until suddenly I would call out with an angry voice directed toward my precious boys. I regretted my aggravated attitude each time afterward, and vowed to always be kind and understanding, and to speak in a loving manner. I decided to change my way of reacting to annoying stimulus. Once I was aware of my unwanted behaviour, I knew it was only a matter of time until I would succeed at changing it. I was creating a new behaviour by learning to discipline my boys while remaining completely relaxed and in a calm state.

Using an example from that morning, I went into meditation and visualized my behaviour of yelling from start to finish. I played it forward and then was guided to play it backward in slow motion as a sort of video, taking note of each step in sequence that needed to be changed. I discovered that just before I yelled, I took a deep angry breath; my irritation growing in intensity as I filled my lungs. Awareness of that deep abrupt breath became the warning to stop myself immediately and exchange it for a conscious, relaxed, slow breath and remove myself from the situation if necessary. Sometimes I would walk into another room for a minute until I could refocus my attention on my goal. At the beginning of my behaviour change, I often became aware of my habit after I had started shouting. Before long I was able to stop myself from yelling altogether as I focused on being aware of the large breath I took just before shouting. Soon I caught my annoyed attitude as it was developing in its early form. Presently I was able to change my irritation into calmness. This arrested my fury, and it wasn't long before the angry thoughts stopped altogether. Shortly after that, I had no irritation anymore with my boys, and I treated them with love and respect. When I had to discipline them I learned to do it in a kind but firm manner. I stopped yelling completely and it felt so wonderful to have accomplished that feat!   Often people unconsciously continue the pattern they learned from their parent's behaviour. When I see people who speak to children and loved ones in a disrespectful manner, I feel very blessed and grateful that I was able to be conscious enough to change my ways.

Many times when faced with a difficult or challenging

situation, and especially when playing back an unresolved challenging event in my mind, I again used the fly-on-the-wall technique to solve or at least try to comprehend what happened. For example, if I had an unpleasant meeting with someone I would recreate that event in my mind, and play it through. Being the observer put me in an unemotional position so I could see the big picture much better. This gave me insight into the other person's perspective and often their motives so I could understand the situation from a universal viewpoint. I frequently found a good solution that could be presented that was mutually beneficial for all people involved. It is so important to remember that each person's perspective is as valid to that person as mine is to me.

Recognizing negative thoughts allows the perfect outlook to release them. Negative thoughts are all thoughts that come from an attitude of less than a state of love. Any thought that lends itself to jealousy, unkindness, meanness, judgment, unforgiveness and so on is not only a negative thought, but it also creates negative karma. That is reason enough to arrest them in their infancy. When a negative thought erupted in my mind, I released it immediately and replaced it with a positive thought

EXERCISES

Manifestation List

A manifestation list is a wonderful tool to help effect desired change in your life. There are many versions of this list, but this is the one I find most helpful.

Write at the top of a piece of paper:

I am so happy and grateful now that:_____

All you have to do is fill in the blank. I put bullet points down the side and add the most pressing things that I want changed in my life first. Some examples of items on my manifestation lists are as follows.

- I have always and only positive thoughts, words and actions.
- I live in the state of love
- I am happy
- I am completely healthy in my mind, body and soul
- I have kind and loving relationships
- I have deep rejuvenating sleep all night long
- I am abundant
- I am organized
- I have firm boundaries
- I exercise daily

Explanation of manifestation sentence:

"so happy": When you emanate emotion to the universe you get a response back. The more emotion you express, the more the universe listens, so generate as much happiness as you can when you read your list at least twice a day.

"grateful": Being in a grateful state of mind creates within you an openness to receiving. If you are asking for things through the Law of Attraction, the Universe can shower you with abundance, but if you are not in receiving mode, these gifts will pass you by.

"now": The universe will give you more of that which you already have. Be grateful for what you do have and choose to have more of it.

Grab and Toss

The Grab and Toss method is easy and quick. It is used

to pluck unwanted thoughts from your mind and negative feelings from your body and especially when I feel a hindrance interfering with my energy flow. It can be used during meditation to remove unwanted thoughts and also during your regular day. Sometimes I become aware of a tight feeling in my gut or in my head or a constricted feeling in my chest and I know the origin is from a negative thought. Subconscious negative energy from the past is triggered from incidents that happen in the present time. This is an opportunity to recognize and remove it. Once you are consciously on your soul path, negativity will keep availing itself for removal. Each time you remove negativity and replenish with light you move one rung higher on your ladder of enlightenment. You can use this exercise to gain more peace in your life. Never underestimate the power of releasing negativity.

Take a few Focused Breaths.

Visualize where that thought is in your body and what it looks like or reminds you of. Usually a thick black cloud or black blob is what I envision. You may or may not see or feel it, but may have an awareness of it. Physically take your hand to that 'cloud,' grab it and toss it to your angels for safe removal. Visualize this as best you can as you don't want negative energy remaining in your surroundings.

Take a deep breath for the void.

Replace the negative thought with the opposite and loving thought. Whenever there is a negative thought, there is a positive replacement. It may take some creativity on your part, but believe me, it does exist. If you can't think of one, replace it with love. Love heals everything. I find that if I put more energy into the positive replacement thought than I put into the original negative thought, it not only feels good, it truly feels that I have righted a wrong and prevented negative karma from forming.

Now, visualize white healing light flowing into you from your Higher Power, filling your body and aura up fully so you are in a large bubble of white healing light. Feel the joy and harmony that it brings to you.

I have done this exercise with many clients and most of them feel the negativity being removed and say they feel much lighter and happier afterward.

CHAPTER 14

CLEARING AND REPLENISHING

There are several steps necessary in order to ascend into a higher state of enlightenment. Negativity needs to be released from all levels; physical, mental, emotional and spiritual, and from all lives.

Excerpt from my On Wings of Love newsletter: *"Clearing and Replenishing - Advance into the Light",* Mar, 2012

Spirit says:

"People, you have chosen to come to Earth at this time to flow with her energy as she ascends. Vast opportunities are now available to release negative karma which will enlighten your soul. Since Mother Earth is travelling now at an increasingly faster rate energetically, this allows the transfer of vibrational energy to be accomplished at an increased pace, more rapidly than any time in the history of Earth. NOW is the time for your progression into the Light; to reunite with Spirit!

In order to climb the Ladder of Enlightenment, it is necessary for you to create for yourself as clear a being as possible. Light must prevail. Therefore as much negativity as possible must be removed from yourself. Then the void must be replaced with Source Light. Removing negativity is similar to the skins of an onion. As you remove the outer skin, the next skin becomes available for removal. This continues on until finally you get to the central core. Once that is removed, there is no more negativity. There is only love.

Releasing negativity/darkness from past and present

will make you feel so much better in all aspects of your life and being. When negativity is removed, a void is created. The Universe doesn't tolerate a void, so it is important to consciously replace the void with Light Energy. Removing negativity in layers is much gentler on the body than removing a lot all at once. When too much negativity is present in the body, people may become ill, in that case, negativity is released through illness. Ailments can come in the form of flu, colds, or more serious diseases and conditions. Learning clearing techniques and performing them regularly can prevent unnecessary dis-ease.

Drawing in Light Energy creates within yourself higher and brighter energy or vibration. Thus you are able to increasingly absorb and hold additional light. This allows you to climb the Ladder of Enlightenment at a progressively faster rate. It helps you to react kindly and with love when challenging situations arise. Light frees your body of darkness so it can heal itself much better. You will enjoy a healthier more energetic mind body and soul. Light carries with it clarity which improves the flow of intuition, and increases your understanding of life circumstances. Light allows you to live a more full and purposeful life, and produces more love, peace and joy in your life. It grants you the power to shine as the bright light that you are.

Negativity can be absorbed into your being from several sources. Negative energy comes from events that happened in your past. If you are unable to repel them, they may be implanted within you in the form of Cell Memory and Pain Bodies. Sensitive and empathic people often take in other people's negative vibration. Guilt, anger, hurt, and emotional pain can be absorbed into the body cells and stored there. Cell Memory and Pain Bodies are also brought forward from past lives. Negativity is very effective in keeping one spiritually, emotionally, mentally and physically stagnant."

I have found for my personal spiritual advancement and my clients', that visualization is a very effective tool for clearing negative energy and replenishing with Light. During many Spiritual Guidance Sessions, the Guardian Angels and Archangels ask me to guide my client through angel healings which inevitably includes clearing of negative energy.

Clearing negativity from yourself will help you receive the guidance system that was created for you. Your guardian angels and teaching angels will be able to communicate with you much more lucidly. You won't necessarily hear their messages in words and sentences, but you will get that distinctive gut feeling that guides you. Clearing helps you to find your Life Purpose and to uncover the True You. That is the soul-you, not the personality you have developed through your ego-mind. Clearing helps your body to become healthier, and have more energy. Your smile becomes a true kind smile that simply with eye contact connects you to people on a much deeper level. It is so wonderful to give and receive soul-felt smiles. Clearing negativity away and bringing in light assists you to rise up the Ladder of Enlightenment. The lighter you become the faster and higher your ascent.

What is negativity and where does it come from? Negativity comes from this life or past lives. It comes from any arguments or disruptions in your life that you were not able to release or forgive completely. This negative or dark energy holds you down, not only in your spiritual endeavours, but in the physical, emotional and mental aspects as well. It causes feelings of heaviness, anxiety, depression, sadness, illness and fear. If you still have any negative emotional feelings from any event that happened in the past, then you haven't released or cleared it from yourself fully.

Negativity attracts more negativity. That is the Law of Attraction. I have seen this first hand many times, but I especially remember a time when I was at work. Five of us were in the lunch room, enjoying each other's company and having a nice chat. In walked the negative employee and immediately she started complaining about her last client and the boss and our receptionist and so on. Before long, the whole group had taken on her darkness and was engaging in negative conversation, empathizing with her recall of the negative events that had preceded lunch. Everyone was being dragged down the negative spiral that she was constructing. I observed this scene with interest. Many times before that day, I had allowed the same co-worker to reduce me down to her level of negativity. This particular day, I offered the simple comment that I was sure that our receptionist was doing the best she could. The co-worker stopped in her tracks, ceased complaining and left the lunch room mystified. Shortly after that day, she quit her job. It was surprising how everyone noticed and commented on how the positive energy at work skyrocketed with her resignation. Several of them exclaimed their relief that they no longer had to tolerate her and her negativity.

When someone is in a negative mood and they have a strong vibration, they are able to project their negativity onto other unprotected beings. Ever wondered why nasty people often have nasty dogs? It is important to protect yourself from negative input. When people are negative it is as if a dark cloud is hanging over them. This dark cloud makes it impossible for their true intuition to be realized. Think of yourself as a radio. If there is a dark cloud around the radio it receives a very fuzzy signal, and if the signal is received at all, it comes through with a lot of static making the message difficult to decipher. Similarly if you have dark energy within and surrounding you, it causes static, and prevents or muffles angelic efforts to communicate with you and guide you. By clearing away the negativity, you become a clear receiver for intuitive signals. A ship in the ocean that has lost its guidance system floats around with no way of knowing which bearing to follow. Similarly people who have lost their ability to communicate with their Higher Power feel that they have no purpose and are wandering around Earth as lost souls with no goal or direction.

Physical illnesses can occur from retained negativity. This can lodge into certain organs, as pain bodies and cell memory. When negative energy is present, your body energy or chi gets blocked and doesn't flow well. Your body becomes unbalanced and your biological systems may become compromised.

People will become educated, read, or do puzzles to improve their cognitive skills and they will eat good healthy food and exercise to improve or maintain their body health. What do they do for their spirit? Mind, Body and Spirit: each one third is just as important as the other two. The majority of people ignore their spirit, so in effect they are ignoring one third of their being. No wonder there is so much illness and dis-ease in this society.

The White Light Tornado Clearing was first revealed to me during a reading. My client was filled with negativity. I was advised to guide her through this meditation and record it so she could refer to it often. Afterward she said that she felt so much lighter and happier. As all clearings, it removes the layers that are ready to be released. This is why it needs to be repeated often, as consecutive layers are then prepared for extraction. When anxiety is felt for any reason, this is a great clearing to do. It can also be used alone, or to clear cell memory and pain bodies.

Cell memory looks to me like dark blocks of similar shape and size to those old fashioned wooden cube and pyramid shaped playing blocks with the letters painted on them. The centrifugal force from the tornado pulls out all these dark blocks of cell memory, and they are dissolved in the white light. Some clients can feel the energy being released; others feel a tingly or light feeling during and after the meditation. Others feel happy and relaxed. Cell memory forms from suppressing negative energy from life experiences that are smaller in nature as opposed to larger negative experiences that cause pain bodies. Cell memory formation could be from an encounter with your boss shouting at you, or if you regretted something you did to a friend or generally from a negative event when you were left feeling moderately upset.

Pain bodies are caused from more potent negative encounters and are much larger in size than cell memory. Pain bodies are formed from absorbing negativity from larger events such as being fired from a job, relationship break-ups, abuse, brutality and generally from a time in your life when you were extremely upset. They appear to me as dark thick tar-like silhouettes of the person, in the form of their whole body or partial body, and sometimes in just one or two chakras. They are anchored into the body by cell memory. Once the cell memory is released, the pain body is removed fairly easily. Pain bodies are caused from suppressing negative energy instead of releasing it. It can be from anytime in the past including past lives. The origin does not matter, they are just as damaging whether they come from past or present lives. Pain bodies can be trapped in organs and especially those that are compromised already by family history from genetics or circumstances. Pain bodies are magnets for negative energy, and releasing them enables you to avoid attracting further dark energy. They are caused from anger, fear, jealousy, guilt, and any negative behaviour from you aimed toward another, from another aimed at you, or from you toward yourself.

I noticed very quickly after I started releasing these unwanted entities that when I was in situations where I would have normally taken in negative energy from another person or setting, I easily refrained from doing so. I was able to remain in my positive outlook. You will create a more uplifting, balanced life with a better attitude, enhanced health and generally a much more positive existence. As you allow more light in, more negativity is brought to the surface so it can be released next. This creates a revolving mechanism that continues until eventually all darkness is released. When you finally reach the inner core and pull that plug out, liberating yourself from all negativity, you feel so amazing; only light remains. The darkness stops controlling, and light guides you through your life with love and kindness, rendering a truly wonderful and generous existence.

EXERCISES

"Clearing": As in all exercises, always ask your angels to help you when doing clearings. They will help you to do a good and thorough task. Be sure to ask them to remove the negative energy to a safe disposal so it is not left hanging around to be absorbed by someone else.

"Void": The Universe doesn't tolerate a void, therefore when you release negativity, take a breath to create a distinct void or vacuum, so when you replenish with light, it comes rushing into you.

"Replenishing": Bring in Universal Light Source into your being by visualizing the brightest and largest light you can imagine. As the sun is to Earth, the Universal Light Source is to the Universe. As long as you state your intention, and do your best visualizing, your angels will do the rest.

White Light Tornado:

Removing Cell Memory

Assume the meditation pose that suits you best and take several Focused Breaths until you are relaxed. Count down slowly from 10 to 1, to take you down into a deep meditative state. Again you can envision yourself going down in an elevator, an escalator or stairs, to descend into a deeper meditation. Go as deep within yourself as possible. The depth you reach will increase with practice.

Say out loud "Angels, help me now to release all cell memory and negativity."

Visualize a long tube about three inches in diameter full of healing light coming to you from Universal Light Source. Light is love. It comes about a meter below your feet and starts spinning a tornado around the outside of your aura. It is beautiful white light that comes to heal you. It spins up to the level of your feet, your knees, hips and all the way up past the top of your head and up just beyond the top of your aura. See this as best as you can.

Feel, see and hear all the blocks being pulled into the tornado by its spinning force. Breathe out all negativity into the light. Remain visualizing here for a few minutes or until you feel you have accomplished the clearing. Visualize that the white light tornado has completely dissolved all the dark blocks into its light. It may help you to think of when a light is turned on in a dark closet, the darkness is completely dispelled. Now the tornado dissolves, but the tube of Universal Light Source remains.

Take a couple of breaths for the void. The Universe always wants to fill a void.

Now see the white light tube entering into either your solar plexus which is the spot just under the sternum, or if you prefer into the top of your head. Envision light flowing through the tube and into you from Source. Feel your body and your whole aura filling up and being saturated with this exquisite healing light. Breathe the bright light into your lungs, soaking it into every cubic millimeter of your whole being. Revel in the glory and peace of the light. Allow it to heal you.

White Light Tornado:

Releasing Pain Bodies

Continue on within the same meditation as started above for removal of cell memory.

Say out loud: "Angels please help me now to release all pain bodies and all negativity." As with everything in your life, your guardian angel finds the appropriate help. The Archangel who is assigned to you will aid with this clearing.

See your Archangel pull the pain body out from your body, usually from your head. Envision him or her pulling the thick black tar-like substance that resembles a silhouette of your body or partial body. It is grabbed and hauled out hand over hand much as a fisherman drags in his fishing net. There may be one pain body that is ready to be released or several, so stay in this part of the meditation until you have allowed enough time for all of the pain bodies to be removed. Usually three to five minutes is sufficient.

Once you feel the pain bodies have been successfully extracted, and have seen them being taken away by an angel for safe disposal, take a couple of breaths for the void. At this point you should feel very peaceful and content.

Replenishing with Healing Light

Your assigned Archangel will replace the void with beautiful healing light.

Visualize your Archangel putting his/her hand either on the top of your head or just below your neck, as he/she transmits personalized specific and superb healing light into your being. See the flow of perfect light filling your body and aura. You may see a colour or have a tingling sensation or a myriad of other delightful responses.

Breathe this beautiful light into your lungs and allow it to permeate you so your whole being is basking in the light. Say: "I accept and receive all healing light." If you speak out loud all your angels can hear you, and help. There are often a substantial number of teaching angels and other light beings assigned to an individual. More angels arrive while healing work is being done. If you speak only in your mind, your Higher Power and guardian angel are the only ones who will be able to hear you and help you.

CHAPTER 15

THE EGO VERSUS THE SOUL

What is the ego? It is the part of the mind that is the root cause of Duality. Duality is the illusion that you are separate from "All There Is" or Creator. There is a better side of the ego and a worse side and everything in between. These two sides of the ego oscillate back and forth as a pendulum, between highs and lows or ups and downs, as on an emotional roller coaster ride. Reducing the power of the ego awakens your true identity, or your soul personality, and your Oneness with your Higher Power or Spirit. Higher Power could be one of or a combination of the following: God, Universe, Holy Spirit, Divine Mother, Jesus, Great Spirit, Buddha or whomever you believe in.

For a simpler discussion, the ego will be divided in half, referring to the pleasant ego and the unpleasant ego. The unpleasant aspect of the ego, which is responsible for the "low wave" of Duality, is the part of your mind where all negativity emerges from. It is the constant chatter. It can be boastful or of low self-esteem. It tells you that you are not enough; not good enough, thin enough, healthy enough, or smart enough. The ego is responsible for all negativity and emotions such as anger, fear, jealousy, racism, selfishness, neediness, sadness, hate, destructiveness and scarcity. It tells you that you're not able to do things that you want to do; you're not strong enough or you don't have time.

The ego resists change and spiritual progress. It interrupts meditation by forming thoughts and distracts you away from what your soul guides you to do. Some people refer to the ego as resistance. The ego resides in either the past or the future, never in the present moment. It regrets things you did or didn't do in the past. It can idolize the past, having you think "If only I could go back there into the past, life was so much better then." The ego also lives in the future, often fearing what is coming up on the horizon. It frequently projects upcoming events to be far worse than they could possibly be, spawning fear and dread of the future. The ego endeavours to occupy your mind and thereby prevents you from living in the present moment. All the enormous benefits of living in the present moment are unavailable while living through the ego.

The pleasant aspect of the ego is responsible for the "high wave" of Duality. It is the part of the mind that is attached to the body and needing to look and feel attractive; it may be vain. It wants to spend time at the hair salon, putting on makeup and trying to look pretty, so it can feel happy when it looks in the mirror. It is attached to material objects, and wants to purchase clothes and items that will satisfy it, or make it look good. The ego wants people to like it, so it may even do somewhat unethical things to fit in with others so it feels a sense of belonging. It may bolster the self-esteem with thoughts of "I'm pretty or handsome," or "I'm better off than that person," or other notions of grandeur that cause conceit. It is always comparing itself to others.

The happiness the ego brings is fleeting. As the body ages or becomes compromised, it no longer brings the happiness it once did. As the clothes and objects get old, they no longer satisfy the ego. When the understanding dawns that teasing someone in order to be accepted by a peer group no longer feels acceptable, the benefit it once brought is lost. The ego only provides temporary gratification.

The pleasant ego is able to perform charitable activities, helping others and making a difference in the world. Because the ego is separate from the whole, when it does good work, there is an element of the self-serving question: "What's in it for me?" or "If I do that for you, then you do this for me." It expects and desires something in return, perhaps receiving some sort of recognition, or even being rewarded for its good deeds. Many egos correctly believe that doing good deeds will afford it a better place in Heaven. However, giving through the ego is not the same as giving from the heart and soul, neither of which requires anything in return. Giving from the heart and soul realizes a much higher place in Heaven.

Giving from the pleasant ego is what creates positive karma. Positive karma as well as negative karma must be released before joining in Oneness with Creator. Oneness is complete when the duelling ego mind is left behind and only the soul with its union to Spirit remains.

In order to move into a state of enlightenment, each person must release the ego and accept and receive the will of Higher Power/Spirit through their soul. Until that intention is declared, the ego will do its best to stay in control displaying all kinds of reasons and ways to 'prove' that it is right. This journey is not for the faint of heart and it is accomplished only with the help from Higher Power and "His" helpers, and angels. It is completely possible and highly rewarding to live your life with no ego, or at least a very reduced ego. It is important to note that releasing the ego, allows the Universal Consciousness to take its rightful place within you. This Spirit-Consciousness is one with the soul; I call it soul-mind and it re-establishes your original connection to the whole, or Oneness. When you live through your soul, you have accomplished the ultimate goal of life on Earth; you have put all of the pieces of the puzzle together. If you return to Earth, you will have an exemplary life, whether you come to help one person or many. Jesus represents the essence of the model we are to follow. He had no ego, and His life and ways are documented for the entire world to read and follow.

What is the soul? The soul is an individual spirit, the spark from Creator. It is consistent, whole, gentle and kind and full of unconditional eternal love. It is the true immortal component of people and all life forms. It is housed temporarily for each lifetime within a body. It resides in any of the chakras, but most often I see it in the solar plexus chakra. The nature of the soul is Spirit; it is eternal, conscious and blissful. The soul is perpetually connected to Spirit. Its purpose is to reunite consciously with Spirit, fully realizing Oneness or wholeness with "All There Is." Living through the soul is accomplished always and only in the present moment. The soul lives in love-light, positivity, peace, wholeness, bliss, understanding, abundance and all good things. Your soul is connected to your Higher Power by a tube of white light. The more you live through the soul, and the more grateful you are, the bigger the tube becomes, and the stronger the connection to Spirit. You are constantly being fed spiritual energy from your Higher Power. The bigger the tube is the more power can come through. Living through the soul creates a joyful life, and offers peacefulness in dealing with challenges. It improves relationships, and helps you to feel that you are never alone; that you belong in this world and in this life. Living through the soul is the basis for creating and existing in Heaven on Earth.

Four Steps to Engage the Soul and Release the Ego:

Recognize - when you are operating through the ego: it is undesirable when you think, speak and act through the ego's negative ways.

182

Accept - that ego is preventing you from attaining your spiritual goals and that you are willing and wanting to change.

Action - modify your behaviour and do exercises that will enable your soul to lead you in a loving and harmonious life.

Awareness - so you keep progressing forward, and not slipping back.

In the Bhagavad Gita, an ancient Hindu Scripture, the battle between the ego and the soul is depicted in a war-scene on a battle field. The story is as valid today as it was thousands of years ago when it was written. The battle goes on and on, with horses and armies, but in the end and what is important is that the ego surrenders to the soul and becomes the soul's meek servant, and becomes complimentary to the soul. The soul leads you in truth, love and harmony. The soul rising above the ego is one of the major factors necessary for merging into the light.

EXERCISES

Purpose: to recognize that the ego is detrimental to your well-being, and to make a conscious decision to surrender your ego to your soul.

Think of an event in your life when something negative happened, and you reacted in a regretful way through the negativity of the ego. It could be an argument with a loved one, anger feelings towards a co-worker, or frustration directed to another person or even a pet.

Awareness: Ego versus Soul

Settle into a light meditation by counting down from 10 to 1 and ask your angels for help.

Go back to that day in your mind. Picture your surroundings, smell the smells, hear the noises, see the other people, animals who were involved and whatever else was there. Feel no emotion: be an observer. Breathe gently.

Now see the negative incident happen. See how you react in a negative way. See all those around you and how your behaviour is affecting them. Notice any guilt or remorse that you feel from this situation and from wishing you had handled it better...much better.

Release

Ask your angels or your Higher Power to fill you with soul feelings of love, forgiveness, non-judgment, peace, understanding, generosity, and kindness. You are now oozing with unconditional love. In this frame of soul-mind visualize the same situation: the negative thing happening and you react in a generous and loving way.

See how those around you are positively affected by your soul light. See how the negative event turns into a compassionate learning experience for everyone involved.

Declaration of Intent

You may want to affirm out loud, as it will make it more real, one or all of the following:

"I now choose to reduce the control my ego has over my soul."

"I invite my soul to be the harmonious leader of my ego."

"I choose to re-establish my soul-mind as it was in the beginning."

"The soul is meant to be the Divine leader of the ego."

Surrendering the Ego to the Soul

Similar to the battle scene in the ancient scriptures, visualize the ego battling the benevolent and neutral soul. The soul, as it is a spark from Spirit, requires no defence. It waits patiently life after life for the release of the ego.

See this as a hologram in front of you: you as your ego which is dressed in black, bent on destroying you as your soul which is dressed in white. I like this done as a one-sided sword fight, but you can choose what feels best to you.

The ego angrily takes its sword and tries to hurt the soul, but the soul, sword-less gently, kindly and firmly stands its ground, and is unhurt by the blow. The frustrated ego raises its sword at a different angle and brings it down on the opposite side of the soul. Once again the soul kindly and lovingly and steadfastly remains, unscathed. This one-sided battle goes on with the soul in its loving state, safe from each strike the ego attempts, patiently awaiting the time that the ego is replaced with Universal Consciousness.

The ego becomes tired and weak, finally realizing that it is no match for the Universal Power. The ego starts to give up. See the ego now shrinking to a small form. The ego now lays its sword down on the ground and kneels in front of the soul. The ego says to the soul: "I am now and forever more your humble servant." Now your soul with its unconditional love and humility arises as the Divine leader of the ego. I call this the soul-mind.

Visualize the shrunken ego being replaced by the Universal Consciousness that is now descending from above as a white light, filling your head, body and aura. Say: "I accept Universal Consciousness now and forever more." Sometimes Universal Consciousness is referred to as "God Consciousness" or "Christ Consciousness."

Enlarging the Soul

Start with the Stillness Within Meditation for several

minutes. Once you can really feel the absolute stillness within, which is your soul energy, start to see, feel, hear and experience your soul. It is often at your solar plexus, just below your sternum. It is about the size of a golf ball or larger. Your soul is the brightest light you could ever imagine.

Visualize the tube of white light connecting your soul to the Universal Light Source, Spirit or your Higher Power. Envision white light flowing through the light tube and into your soul. Now see that golf ball of light getting bigger...it is now the size of a tennis ball and still growing. It is expanding to the size of a basketball, and now a large beach ball. The light keeps enlarging until it fills your body and your whole aura.

See the circumference of the tube of light spreading at the same rate as your soul increases in diameter. Soon it is a huge beam of light – as large as your aura, and it is pouring white light all around you. Feel the love, joy, bliss, abundance and all goodness that the light contains. This is the way we are meant to be living – in this beautiful state of unconditional love. Breathe deeply and enjoy this magnificent feeling for a while. See how long you can keep this beautiful feeling throughout your day.

CHAPTER 16

PRESENT MOMENT

Excerpt from my *On Wings of Love* newsletter *"Present Moment"*, Feb. 2012

"When I ask people what they want most in life, very often the answer is: "I just want to be happy!" When living through the Ego-mind and all its negativity, happiness is very fleeting. Some people try to find happiness from purchasing material objects: a new wardrobe, a new bike or car. Happiness cannot be bought! Similarly, many people think and hope that they can find happiness through a relationship with someone who will "make them happy". When that partner fails to deliver, which sooner or later they always will, the person becomes disillusioned with the relationship and may move on to another relationship, and then another, and so on. No one can make you do anything, much less make you happy. These cycles continually repeat themselves until finally the person realizes that happiness cannot be attained from material objects or from other people. Happiness cannot be found from external sources. True lasting happiness is only attained from within. Inner joy is generated from being on the path to Oneness with Creator, and by living through the soul in a state of love.

Once one is ready for spiritual advancement many questions arise. "Who am I? What am I doing here? Is there something more to life that I'm missing? Have I come for some purpose and if so what is it?" Many other similar life questions emerge. Often there is an inkling of some inner knowing that there is much more out there...somewhere. We have a strong desire to tap into this information, but don't know how, or even where to start looking for it. It is an innate feeling that you are always searching for something that will allow you to feel like you belong, that you have a purpose, or that you are a part of something big and powerful and meaningful. Only through Spirit does one find the answers to life's big questions. This is a search for the Ultimate Truth: a truth you can believe in absolutely without a doubt, when you discover it.

The journey to Enlightenment is the journey to Truth. It can help to answer soul-driven questions, giving you a peaceful and all-encompassing understanding of life. As negativity is released, your true personality is revealed: "The True You" or your Soul Personality.

One of the common Soul Purposes we come to Earth to accomplish is to reunite with Spirit. Once this goal is intended, you are able to start experiencing elements of Oneness with All There Is. Intention is very powerful. Intention begins the forward motion that induces creating or remembering and living your individual Soul Purpose.

The ego-mind is attached to time and cannot function in the present moment: it only operates in the future and the past. The soul however resides in the spiritual realm and follows the universal agenda and is independent of Earth time. It is therefore only accessible to you when you are in the Present Moment. Therefore when your awareness is in the moment, you are in your soul space. To start moving your life towards residing in your soul, it is important to learn how to do simple daily tasks while in the Present Moment. The more you do this, the more it becomes a habit. More tasks can be added to your soul space repertoire, and soon you will be living a greater amount of time in this peaceful and loving state. What used to be perceived as difficulties, become opportunities to grow. Intuition becomes much clearer, and beauty is seen in everything around you."

Heightened awareness is experienced during the state of being in the Present Moment. It is awareness of self and of Spirit. All external things fade into the background. Your consciousness is focused within your Being. Co-ordinating movement with breath is a simple way to be in the moment. Yoga is a good example of this; during postures, the focus is on breathing into your body and movement. When you focus on your breath it brings you into the moment. If you are in a thought, past or future, you are not focusing on your breath, and are not in the moment. If it sounds simple it is because it is. Look for the simple things in life, because that is where Oneness and Enlightenment are. Wherever you are, and whatever you are doing, you can bring yourself back immediately into the present moment by focusing on your breath.

Mindfulness is a practice of being in the moment. After learning the following meditations and visualizations, you will be able to bring Mindfulness into your daily life, you will discover after a short time that you are beginning to live through your soul. Your soul will expand to encompass all aspects of your life. It starts to become your natural way of existence. Mindfulness leads to happiness, joy, peace, understanding, and abundance in all good things.

Because of our ego-based society, we live in a world of duality. That is the world of opposites. Examples are high and low, fast and slow, light and dark, love and hate, pleasure and pain. As a pendulum swings back and forth, so does the amount of pleasure and pain in similar amounts. As stated before, it can feel like an emotional roller coaster. I repeat that one common example of duality is when people think that acquiring material objects will bring them happiness. They hope that buying a new jacket or pair of shoes will bring them joy. When that brief happiness wanes, they may become depressed or sad. Then they buy another item that they think will bring them happiness. The pattern repeats itself until the person realizes that the old saying: "money can't buy happiness" is true. Ego-induced attempts to find happiness are doomed to failure. No one can "make" you happy, or for that matter no one can make you sad, angry or miserable. Your reactions to stimuli are your choice. Make them conscious decisions.

When you release the ego and live through the soul, you transcend the world of duality. True inner soul experiences are aligned with your Higher Power. They have no opposites. That is why when living through the soul you can be in a constant state of bliss. During or soon after developing the ability to dwell in the soul, awareness of your Life Purpose evolves. Necessary building blocks for your purpose start to line up and are presented in various ways and forms.

Summary: How do I live in the present moment? Being focused on your breath brings you into the present moment... always. Focus on breath=being in the present moment=living through your soul=happy life. It's as simple as that. Learning how to focus on breath is best taught in a breathing meditation. How do I reunite with Spirit? Live through the soul! When you are consciously living through your soul you are fully with Spirit.

EXERCISES

Life Force Meditation

Start with the Focused Breath and count from 10 to 1 into your meditation and ask your angels for help.

As you breathe, think about how air sustains life. It is not just air you are breathing, it is Life Force. Life Force is light energy which includes the properties for healing, clearing, love, joy peace. The Sanskrit name for Life Force is Prana.

Take this active Prana into your body and heal yourself. Notice any discomfort or stiffness in your body. It can be visualized as a dark blob. Breathe Life Force into that area. Envision that area being filled with white light healing energy. See the dark blob transmuting from darkness into light. Release the discomfort through your exhalation. With the next breath, fill that area with white light again, healing it completely.

To heal emotional pain, visualize a dark shadow that represents an emotional issue covering your body. If you feel negative energy in a specific area of your body you may envision the shadow there. Fill the shadow and your body with light. See the light infusing the darkness. Healing can be accomplished by breathing light into any problems you are having, be it emotional, mental, spiritual or physical.

Now, see the life force entering the brain, feeding it and healing it. Visualize your brain power increasing and your memory and cognitive skills augmenting. Envision your red blood cells picking up oxygen from your lungs and carrying it to, and healing every part of your body. See your body being lit up like a light bulb with the healing energy of life force. Remain in this meditative state for a while.

Mindfulness Meditation

When you are ready, stay in the meditative state described above and s l o w l y open your eyes, to a soft gaze looking in front of you at the floor. Keep focusing on your breath. If you start to come out of the meditative state, you may need to close your eyes for a while as you refocus and get back into your meditative state. Then slowly open your eyes again.

You must be able to function with your eyes open while you are focused on your breath. We are about to do an exercise that will add simple tasks to your soul work. At first it is easiest to do the simple tasks while in a meditative state. After a short time, you will be able to live through your soul, doing small tasks while fully awake. To live through the soul, it is important to bring present mindedness into your everyday life. This is a conscious choice to live in happiness, joy, peace, and all abundance.

The soul is connected to a Higher Power by a string or tube of white light. The more you live through the soul, the bigger the tube becomes, and the stronger the connection to Spirit. You are constantly being fed spiritual energy by your Higher Power. The bigger the tube is, the more power can come through.

Mindfulness Walking Meditation

This is a great way to bring the soul and the present moment into your everyday life. Choose an activity that is mindless, meaning that it is easy to do and you don't have to think about it. For most people, walking is fairly automatic. Dishwashing, hanging laundry, gardening, eating, are also simple tasks that do not engage the mind much. Anything that needs brain power such as reading, writing, mathematics, computer work, driving, talking and listening are not suitable.

Remain in silence. Stand and do a few Focused Breaths while you count from 10 to 1 into a meditation for several minutes. When you feel you are ready, slowly open your eyes to a gentle gaze on the floor in front of you while remaining focused on your breathing. Breathe rhythmically. At any time if you feel yourself coming out of meditation, close your eyes and focus on your breath. This allows you to go back into a deeper meditative state. Then gently continue your soul work.

Start to walk extremely slowly by putting your heel on the floor, rolling your foot forward and onto the ball of your foot, and onto your toes. Keep focused on every component of what you are doing. Say in your mind: I am now putting my right heel on the floor. I am now rolling my weight forward to the ball of my foot. I am now moving forward onto my toes. I am now bringing my left foot forward. I am now putting my left heel on the floor; I am now rolling my left foot forward to the ball of my foot...and so on. It is such a slow walk that you have lots of time to keep a continual commentary about what you are doing. If your mind is busy it cannot wander and it remains focused on the NOW. Slowly swing your arms, and really focus on all the muscles, bones and all the body parts you utilize to do this very measured walk. Notice your balance or imbalance walking at such a slow pace. As you become more disciplined, you will not have to comment about your actions as much, because your mind will not wander as much. Some days you will be able to focus better than others.

Soon you can walk at a faster rate, focusing on larger movements, alternating with the super slow walk. Co-ordinate breath with movement, as this helps to keep you in the moment so the running commentary is not as necessary. I find this much more rewarding. Take a breath in, as you step one foot forward, and release that breath as you bring the other foot forward, completely focused on your body and the movement.

There are many tasks you can do during your daily life to bring you into the moment and into your soul. Be creative. I choose easy tasks for myself, things I can do almost automatically. By bringing mindfulness to your day, you live through your soul and begin the transcendence from the world of duality and start to live in Oneness or Heaven on Earth.

Mindfulness - Small Task

Take a few Focused Breaths, and come into a quiet relaxed mode. As you do your task, say what you are doing over and over in your mind as your body does the corresponding action. By repeating the word now often, it reminds you that you are in the moment or in the "now".

Some examples of what I do:

Washing dishes: I am now washing the front of the plate. I am now washing the back of the plate. I am now rinsing the plate. I am now placing the plate in the dish rack. I am now washing the inside of the cup. I am now washing the outside of the cup. I am now rinsing the cup. I am now placing the cup in the dish rack... I am now washing the spoon. I am now...

Folding laundry: I am now folding the towel in half. I am now folding the towel in half again. I am now placing the towel in the pile of laundered towels. I am now picking up the t-shirt from the laundry basket. I am now folding the t-shirt in half. I am now......

Pouring tea: I am now grasping the handle of the tea pot. I am now pouring the tea into the tea cup. I am waiting for the tea to steep. I am now watching the steam as it rises from the cup. I am now bringing the tea cup to my lips. I am now sipping the tea. I am now putting the tea cup on the saucer. I am now picking up the tea cup again...

Eating dinner: I am now picking up my fork. I am now placing food on my fork. I am now bringing the fork to my lips. I am now putting the food into my mouth. I am now putting the fork on the plate. I am now chewing my food. I am very grateful for this food. I am now picking up the fork again...

For any of these tasks, once you can focus on the task and stay in the moment, try coordinating your movement to your breath, as we did in the walking exercise.

So remember wherever you go and whatever you are doing if you are stressed and obviously not in the moment, consciously take a big belly breath and focus intently on the task you are doing.

CHAPTER 17

ACCEPTING WHAT IS

Excerpt from my *On Wings of Love* newsletter *"Accepting What Is"*, June, 2012

"When you live in complete acceptance of what is, that is the end of all drama."

Eckhart Tolle

"I am a lover of what is, not because I am a spiritual person, but because it hurts when I argue with reality." Byron Katie

"Accepting what is creates harmony in your life. Non-acceptance of what is creates pain in your life. Which one do you prefer? Acceptance of what is means you fully accept that a situation is happening or that a person is the way he or she is. More generally, you accept all aspects of your life as it is. There is no judgment. Forgiveness is an act of acceptance. To accept is not to condone. These are two different concepts. Condoning means that you agree with what is happening. Accepting what is, even though you disagree with it, may be quite challenging. Acceptance comes from a soul-based personality. Finding the root fear of why you resist acceptance of what is, brings an understanding of, and insight into the deeper issues that are contributing to the present situation. Once this root fear is released, the obstacle is overcome much more easily. Then you can move forward, infusing positive energy into the situation which can create a peaceful and harmonious solution. If an argument between two people surfaces and one person stops the negative energy input, the other person has no resistance to support his or her negative energy. The argument is arrested. Resolving the issue then becomes the focus. Similarly, surrendering the situation to your Higher Power releases resistance and dissolves the deadlock created by the negative energy. Only then the situation changes for the better. There are many methods designed to uncover the reasons for resistance and to give understanding to the root issues. Awareness and understanding behaviour is the key to changing it.

Often we are blind to our resistance of what is. The cause of a large majority of emotional pain is due to the non-acceptance of what is. When you go against what is, there is no peace or harmony. Non-acceptance breeds fear, judgment, control, anger, anxiety, panic, and other negative feelings, behaviour and actions. Dwelling on unmet expectations is not accepting what is. Having expectations most often leads to disappointment. What is, *is* the Truth; it *has* happened, or that person *is* that way. Resisting what is, means you are in denial of what is, and therefore pain evolves, and no good solutions to problems can be found. Trying to control a person or situation comes from ego-mind based personalities. Sometimes control emerges from wanting to protect loved ones from what we fear will be unpleasant experiences. Challenging life experiences are prescribed to teach everyone involved lessons of great magnitude.

When complete and consistent acceptance for past, present and future is accomplished, life is peaceful and harmonious. There is nothing that can ruffle your feathers. Instead of travelling on the emotional roller coaster of life, you will be floating on the calm waters of the Lake of Peace and Tranquillity."

Virtually all emotional pain comes from non-acceptance of what is. Think about it. Remember the last time that you were in an emotional upheaval and how long it lasted. Once you finally accepted the situation, the emotional pain dissolved. Unfortunately, for some people it is so difficult to accept certain situations that they never get to the part where they dissolve the pain. They carry emotional pain for the rest of their lives. The accumulation of unresolved negativity penetrates the being and over time causes dis-ease.

Abuse is never tolerated. Once an abused person, for example a woman, accepts that the negative behaviour is happening, then she can move forward and find a solution to the issue. While she is in a state of denial, her situation is static; there is no forward motion to free her from the mistreatment.

EXERCISE

Think of an event or something that has happened in your life that has some negative energy surrounding it. It could be a person who you have not accepted yet. It may be anger, sadness, frustration or other negative thoughts that you feel when thinking about a particular issue. We are working toward bringing this event or person into acceptance rendering your life more peaceful and harmonious. Remember, accepting only means that you accept that something happened - therefore what is. It does not mean that you agree with any thoughts, words or actions of your own or others.

Movie Theatre

Take some Focused Breaths, and count from 10 to 1 and descend into a deep meditative state and ask your angels for help. For the purpose of this exercise, I will use the example of a person who you have not accepted or someone whose ideas or behaviour has been unacceptable to you so far.

Think about the person who you are having negative emotions about. Remember a specific event when something unacceptable happened between you two, and feel all the negative emotions that arose within you. Now in your mind visualize that same scene. Pretend you are seated in a theatre watching a movie or play of this event. See yourself as the actor who is playing your role in this scene. The other person is playing his role and anyone else who was involved is also in the performance. View the movie or play from beginning to end, incorporating everything that happened. Doing this helps you to leave the emotion with the actors and you can see the whole event from beginning to end with little or no emotional reactions. This is a form of the fly-on-the-wall technique described earlier and helps you to see the bigger picture. Seeing *is* believing. When you see in your visualization that which is true and has happened, you realize that it *is.* There is no way of denying the truth and being harmonious, so acceptance becomes achievable.

It may be helpful to envision the same scene a few times to accept the situation fully and see everyone's reactions from a neutral perspective. The next step is to release all judgment and forgive everyone involved in the event.

CHAPTER 18

FORGIVENESS AND NON-JUDGMENT

I found in my personal life that unforgiveness was holding me back from emotional well-being and from moving forward spiritually. There were several instances in my life starting from my childhood that required forgiveness of myself and others. Once this was accomplished by following the exercises below, I was relieved to find that in new, similar situations I no longer judged and was able to forgive quickly and easily. Awareness is the key. My life took on a whole new positive energy at this point and I began to see light and goodness in everyone, even if their light was covered with many layers of blockages. Forgiveness for self and others for all past indiscretions is necessary as retaining these only increases the negativity within and attracts more negativity to you, and allows darkness a foothold in your life.

Excerpt from *On Wings of Love* newsletter, *"To Forgive is Divine"*, May, 2013

"If people truly forgave their selves and others, they would be so full of light it would feel as if the weight of the world was lifted from them."   Mary Anne Johnston

"Forgiveness is one of the necessary elements for developing Oneness with All There Is. Forgiveness is the key that opens the door to the higher aspects of awareness and ultimately to enlightenment. Forgiveness is the essence of light which develops into Divine or Whole love. It is the essential ingredient that allows soul-based unconditional love to surpass ego-based conditional love.

Forgiveness is selfless and kind. It is loving and full of humility. It is uplifting and creates such a feeling of unconditional love within. Once forgiveness is complete, you will feel such an overwhelming love for the 'forgiven'. Forgiveness goes hand-in-hand with unconditional love. You can't have one without the other.

Acceptance allows for non-judgment, which allows forgiveness. Forgiveness is the key to opening the heart which then brings forth peace and tranquillity. Peace promotes love and living in a state of love, which transcends into joy. Joy develops into bliss which in essence is Oneness with Creator and the entire Universe. These are the elements which create within yourself the vibration necessary to heal yourself of all your ailments physically, emotionally, mentally and spiritually. The following step is to heal your immediate environment, resurrecting Heaven on Earth. Expanding the energy in turn allows you to heal the world back into its bountiful peaceful original condition. This is possible if we all do our part.

How do I forgive someone who has upset me?

'Love your enemy.' Projecting love to your enemy - meaning the person you want to forgive - will start the process of forgiveness. This can be done remotely and effectively while you are in a quiet space, or in meditation. It is important to be *willing* to forgive. That is all you really need. Ask for help from your angels and allow yourself to release the judgment. If you have trouble with that, here are some concepts that might help.

Know that there is a huge universe of which we only are able to see and understand a very minute amount through the tunnel vision that we are permitted. There is a much bigger picture that none of us can see, and it is very valid and worthy. Everything happens for a purpose, even though we can't see or understand the purpose, know that it does exist and is extremely important; accept that this *is*.

Recognize that you know nothing of what another person's perspective is or where and why it originated. It is not necessary or even likely that you can fully step into their shoes and understand their thought process and their words or actions.

Understand that another person's perspective is just as valid to him/her as your perspective is to you. No one's perspective is right, and no one's perspective is wrong. It just *is*.

Give people the benefit of the doubt. Everyone does the best they can with what they have. It is not your job to judge others. Remember that forgiving does not mean that you condone or agree with what has been done. It just means that you release yourself and others from your judgment of what has been done.

Unforgiveness only hurts you. The other person is often oblivious to your thoughts, feelings, anger or frustration. These are *your* negative energies and they affect *your self*. They are very demoralizing and debilitating and prevent you from feeling and increasing love within. Visualizations in which the focus is forgiving yourself and others can be learned and practiced. This will help you to move forward on your path."

Forgiveness is such an important aspect of self-mastery that I want to emphasize its magnitude. Through forgiveness alone, one can manifest enlightenment. It is the one Divine tool that we have been given that has far-reaching effects. If you are able to forgive, you are able to love unconditionally. Unconditional love is dependent on forgiveness, and the two are dependent upon each other. If you are able to forgive people whom you have negative feelings toward, then you can advance to the next steps which are to bring acceptance and then love into your heart for them and for yourself. When you have accomplished this, you have unconditional love which is the pathway to enlightenment.

So many people ignore this most important opportunity. Since nothing in the Universe is a coincidence, why do you think there are people who challenge you in your life? It is to provide chances for you to enhance your forgiveness ability and to create unconditional love. The universe always provides whatever it is that you need for your spiritual growth. Realize your opportunities and be grateful for them. In fact, be grateful for all the people in your life with whom you have a challenging relationship, whether you know them personally or if you only know them through the media. It could be someone on the other side of the world who is stirring up your emotions and giving rise for you to assign judgment. Forgiveness is the key to living in the state of love. Accept others for who they are and for their purpose which they are learning and remembering.

All people have the right to exercise the Law of Free Will and it is important to accept this fact. Once forgiveness and acceptance are fully applied, amazing solutions to problems will erupt within you. Resolutions are hidden while you are upset but are frequently so obvious once the blockages have been released. Your relationship with the person will rise to a new and acceptable level. As for the people who cause havoc onto the masses, sometimes the only thing we can do is send love to them. The reason why terrorists cause so much devastation is because they have no love within themselves. This is also true for criminals, whether in jail or at-large or still working in their cushy jobs. If we send love to them and they absorb enough of it, they will at the very least soften their attitude toward others and possibly and hopefully rise to a higher vibration, changing their outlook and behaviour for the better.

To live in the state of forgiveness, recognize when someone displays behavioural characteristics that would normally allow tension to develop within you. As you feel that old deep-rooted energy at the very beginning stage, do a Focused Breath to centre yourself into your soul space. Know with deep conviction that you have the intention to accept and forgive all behaviours. Consciously react lovingly, kindly but firmly to the stimuli. Responding in this way is the road toward living in the state of love. Once you are willing to start the process of forgiving and accepting, change will begin to happen. While you are non-forgiving and projecting judgment onto another, the energetic field between the two of you is static and unchanging. Once one of you exchanges static for clarity, you can begin to see the bigger picture, meaning you can see your way to a better choice and find a better solution, creating change in a positive direction. Opportunities will present themselves for your appraisal.

Living in the state of forgiveness is when you accept all others for who they are and for their purpose whether you agree with them or not. It is forgiving all situations in life before during and after you have become aware of them and therefore having an all-encompassing vibration of forgiveness that precedes you. People can feel this energy being projected toward them, and will subconsciously react to it and become much more forgiving themselves. You can change your environment and the people you come in contact with in a positive way. By bringing forgiveness into another's energy field, that person in turn will project this same energy to those with whom he is in contact with and the results can be large and life-changing. If many people did this, the world would transform to a more kind and loving planet.

True forgiveness is only possible when there is no judgment. It is so important to be non-judgmental in your outlook and attitude in life for yourself and others. If you have no judgment, you are living in a state of forgiveness. Forgiveness is held in high esteem and is a necessary step on the path to enlightenment. Judgment is rampant these days and unfortunately many institutions rely on judgment to keep their members in line. Often religious beliefs include ideas that *their* religion is the only way to salvation. This often gives the followers cause to feel superior to people of other religions, even to the point in severe cases, to cause death to people of other religious beliefs. One example of judgment within religion and race is when people are forced to marry someone within their affiliation or race as opposed to marrying for reasons of love and compatibility.

Prospect for judgment arises during an average day in many ways. Perhaps you assign judgment when you are driving, someone cuts you off and you have to slam on the brakes or swerve to avoid an accident. Maybe you get to work and someone has taken your usual parking spot and you make a judgment against that person. Next your boss gives you extra work to do when you already have a full schedule. The new employee made the coffee way too strong. By the time it's 10:00 am, you could have made many judgments. What goes around comes around is an old saying. Some people refer to it as negative karma or drawing negativity to yourself through the Law of Attraction. Conversely if you live your life from your soul consciousness through love and forgiveness, you will not be attracting any more negativity.

EXERCISES

Forgiving Yourself

Go into this exercise with the intention of forgiving yourself. Think of a situation in which you have been unforgiving of something that you did or didn't do. For the first time through this exercise, pick an event that is mildly irritating and leave major emotionally charged circumstances for when you are more practiced. You are going to have a conversation with your Higher Power. This can be whoever you feel comfortable with. For the purpose of this exercise, I will refer to your chosen being as a male Higher Power.

Take a Focused Breath and go into a light meditation. You are now facing your Higher Power. Feel the love and forgiveness that your Higher Power has for you. Explain the situation that you want forgiveness for. Include as many details as necessary and tell the story from beginning to end. Know that He understands you completely. See, hear and feel Him project immense love and forgiveness to you. Your Higher Power always forgives you for everything. Envision yourself sitting across from your Higher Power as He tells you: "You are perfect. I love you unconditionally." He may have an additional message for you, or you may feel light and tingly. You now feel overwhelming forgiveness for yourself. Sit here for a while in the presence of your Higher Power, basking in His intense energy.

You may choose to ask forgiveness from or apologize to a person who was involved with your above situation or for a different situation all together. You can do this in person if it is a wise option. If not, you can speak to 'him' remotely by speaking to a photo of that person or visualizing them. I have often used a stuffed toy with the person's name pinned onto the toy. Speak from your heart. The person will feel your intention subconsciously through the ethers. Next time you meet him it will be a much less charged interaction than it would have been otherwise.

Forgiving Another

Think of a specific scene that you can recreate for your visualization. It is an occasion in which you felt and still feel unforgiveness and judgment toward another person.

Take some Focused Breaths as you descend into a meditative state.

Bringing all the senses into the visualization makes it more real and therefore creates a much better opportunity for releasing judgment and instilling forgiveness. Re-live the situation fully. Hear all the sounds that were present. Smell any odours that were present at the time. Taste any food or drink that was available at the setting. Touch anything that was there. For example if the situation happened at a dinner party, see yourself sitting at the table. Hear the drone of the people's conversations, smell the food, taste the drink, feel the fork and knife in your hands. Fully sense that you are in that same situation again.

Envision the person who you are forgiving and see the disharmonious interval from beginning to end. Recreate the scene as accurately as possible. Take a few breaths when you are finished.

Next, visualize that you are standing beside your Higher Power. *Feel* the unconditional love and forgiveness your Higher Power has for you. Replay the same scene as if it was a movie and you and your Higher Power are watching it. You now have no emotional attachment to the scene from this place of peace as you are observing from the 3rd person. Feel the love your

Higher Power has for all people including the people in your movie.

Now step into the body of the person you haven't forgiven and replay the movie. Be an actor in the movie playing that person. Feel what that person felt, see everything from her perspective. What is she thinking? How is she feeling? What are her needs? Use your generous and compassionate intuitive imagination.

Next visualize the unforgiven sitting, facing her Higher Power in conversation. Know that at all times the unforgiven is doing the best she can with what she has. Envision her Higher Power loving her unconditionally and feel that love. Sense the forgiveness and non-judgment that her Higher Power has for her and bring her viewpoints into your consciousness. You now are able to bring forgiveness for her into your own consciousness. You may need to repeat this exercise to remove all unforgiveness if it is deep-rooted.

Releasing the past generates freedom for the present and future!

CHAPTER 19

FREEDOM AND NON-ATTACHMENT

Many people create for themselves a prison where they must conform to the rules and regulations that they consciously or subconsciously have set for themselves. These rules may have been taught to them by society, parents, spouses, care-givers, teachers, past lives or simply their own fear. Many people are afraid of being free and of all the responsibility that they imagine it would bring. Nothing could be farther from the truth. Freedom is releasing oneself from the burdens of captivity thereby opening the door to enlightenment, in-dependence and forward motion on all levels. This increases the ability to utilize the Universal Law of Free Will. Once free will is attained, the Law of Attraction is accessible to a much larger degree. Life can then be constructed into a truly ideal existence.

Freedom

One morning as I was in the twilight zone of being half asleep and half awake, I was experiencing a recurring dream about me being locked in a prison cell. There were no other prisoners in the jail, and there was a male warden who pos-sessed the key to my cell. I silently looked him in the eye and he knew he had to open the cell door, which he did promptly. Without speaking, he escorted me down the hallway, unlocked the main door of the prison and released me into the court-yard. He then escorted me to the main gate and opened it. I exited the prison without delay. I walked for a few seconds, realized I was free and started running as fast as I could, afraid they would come after me and imprison me again. I awoke at this point, knowing that no-one was tracking me down, and that it was a self-imposed prison from which I escaped. It was quite a revelation for me. Up until this point I was oblivious to the fact that I had been living in such limitation all my life. All of a sudden the truth was staring me in the face. I had not remembered the previous similar dreams in my wakened state. They were only revealed to me while I was in my half-asleep state. Since there are no coincidences and I know that recurring dreams are very significant, I asked the angels to help me process this new discovery.

I was guided to recreate this dream including all details in a visualization, but with great emphasis and determination to be free. My dream became my inspiration to acquire freedom. It was the beginning of the process of freeing me from all that I had imprisoned myself with. During the visualization I amplified the end of my dream by having a horse at the prison gates, so I could gallop off into the sunset along the sandy road that led from the prison up the hill into the most beautiful green meadow, where I felt love and joy and freedom as never before. It was a beautiful sensation, one that I chose to continue and enhance.

Over the next few weeks, I kept asking for help to recognize and release any and all restrictions so I could become free in all aspects. Once I was aware of the feeling of being free I was able to identify the feeling of being limited, and was capable of releasing that which was confining me by referring to my clearing and replenishing techniques.

I learned that freedom needs to be attained on all levels: physical, mental, emotional and spiritual. Freedom must be cultured in relationships with self, and with others.

One must have the power to make choices that are best for all concerned. It is necessary to be and feel safe and secure on all levels at all times in order to evolve into freedom.

Non-Attachment

Freedom is never truly acquired until non-attachment is conquered. Non-attachment is vital, because with attachment, one is still chained to the third dimensional desire of acquiring more worldly things. This includes but is not limited to money, material objects, love, sex, affection, alcohol, drugs, and other addictions. In addition to being needy for the aforementioned things, the desire to be needed by others is also a strong attachment and a deterrent to spiritual growth. Attachment is the equivalent of mental poverty. Once I fully realized that I had and would always have everything I needed, as was my true right as a child of God/Universe, I was able to overcome my attachment in all aspects. This in turn allowed me to manifest even more independence and true abundance, and brought me into a higher state of consciousness. Non-attachment is liberating; it is to be alright with all the human entrapments and alright without them.

Attachment comes in many forms. For example people are sometimes attached to a certain social status. Unfortunately our society holds money in high esteem which often generates greed and rivalry. This in itself causes separateness in that one believes himself to be of greater or lesser importance than others. Separateness can also be produced because of one's perception that he holds a superior career. Many times professionals and high income earners and their families think of themselves as being better than the majority of society. Their personalities and self-worth are attached to money and material objects. Equally toxic is one who believes himself to be less than others; perhaps because of lack of money, job, status or love. These people are attached to poverty and lack of material objects. The truth is that no one is worth more or less than anyone else to the Universal Consciousness. The street person is just as important to Spirit as the CEO of a highly profitable company.

Some people are attached to drugs and alcohol through addiction. This largely prevents them from following their spiritual paths. Their body chemistry is being altered away from that which was created in perfection by Creator. Poor decisions emerge that inhibit them from following their soul path. Drugs block intuition and soul guidance. The addict remains on a continual circle off of their soul path until they release themselves from the addiction. At that point they are given opportunities and encouragement that will help them to navigate back onto their path and move forward on their spiritual journey.

Individuals are often attached to their body in an exaggerated way. One of the common soul purposes is to dutifully take care of the body by feeding it well, exercising it moderately, keeping it clean, and giving it what it requires for well-being. However, some people are over-the-top in their desire to have what they perceive as either an attractive or an unattractive body. Sometimes one engages in cosmetic surgery for the enhancement of physical attractiveness. When this occurs one is negating and hijacking Creator's perfect design. There is good reason why we choose our particular body, which may not be readily apparent. Our body choice enhances the life path we have chosen to follow, and augments our effectiveness on Earth. The body is after all the envelope or robe that allows the soul to access this world and perform the purpose for which we are here. Conversely some people choose to grossly overeat purposely to create a body that will be unattractive. They may be socially awkward and don't want attention especially from the opposite sex. It is more comfortable for them to avoid an invitation for a date by being unattractive than to risk painful communication with an admirer and decline an overture. Some people are attached to harming their bodies by over-eating or under-eating, over-exercising or under-exercising, and forms of self-mutilation, all of which cause unhealthy results.

Many people are attached to being in a relationship and therefore remain in undesirable relationships. This can be for several reasons, for instance, the fear of living alone, not wanting to rock the boat, not wanting to hurt feelings, a desire or need to be taken care of, lack of funds, apathy, religious reasons, sacrificing themselves to the partner, and settling for who is available and not wanting to wait any longer for Mr. or Mrs. Right to show up. Relationships entered for inappropriate reasons result in lots of unhappiness.

Conversely when a relationship is begun and lived through selflessness, purity of love, respect, and non-attachment, it has a strong propensity to lead to Whole or Divine relationship. Freedom from neediness and dependency on a partner creates a love bond like no other. Two people are choosing to have a partnership because they love each other and want to create an exceptional union.

Freedom can be exercised also through everything you do. Work can be seen as a positive choice where you work at a job you like because you want to have the resources to live a good life and be helpful in society. Conversely, living in a state of neediness would tend to be seen as a negative choice where you work at a job you don't like, because you are afraid of lack of money. If you feel you are obliged to do something, or it is expected of you, change your attitude to wanting to help and be productive in society. Intention is everything, and these examples of differences in attitude cannot be understated. It is the difference between living a free and joyful life as opposed to an attached depressed life.

Again, recognizing your unwanted personality traits is the key to removing them. Releasing myself from neediness was a fairly intricate and diverse process which I am still working with, but basically when I get a tight feeling in my abdomen or heart or a feeling of uneasiness, I use the "grab and toss" procedure described previously. Often I would grab and hold while I deliberated the cause of the restriction before tossing it; I found this method most useful. In pondering situations, I often became insightful of similar neediness that could be removed simultaneously. Because attachment was so ingrained in my personality, its full release was aided by processing where and why the neediness originated. It's not necessary to study all the details and circumstances which created the negativity, however it is essential to be willing let it go. Following the release, I always filled myself with healing light from source.

During my long career as a health care provider I was often subjected to emotional pain that my patients were feeling. Unfortunately, the negative energy of these people from all walks of life was affecting me immensely. I knew I had to find a way to not take on this vibration. Immunity is a concept that came to me when I finally realized how much the negative energy of patients was affecting me adversely. I was taking this energy home with me to my family as well. Even though I protected myself and put a shield around me, the energy was attaching itself to me. In retrospect, I concluded that through my sympathy I was welcoming clients' energies to enter my auric field. After listening to a commercial for a television show about survival, I decided to ask for immunity to negative vibes, tongue in cheek. To my surprise I was shown a series of steps to follow that would guarantee that I would not take in any more negative energy.

I was shown a scene in a museum where the patrons were invited to touch articles. The articles were in a box made of clear glass that had small arm holes so I could put my hands inside to feel the items. I could not take these larger items out of the box through the smaller holes. I was to simulate this in the following manner. I was to allow my empathic receptors to experience how a client was feeling and then retract my receptors, leaving the energies within that person. This was quite different than what I had been doing subconsciously before. Some of the energies would remain within me, leaving me sad, lonely and angry as I became weary and burdened. The clients felt much better and would suddenly feel happy and relieved, but it was unhealthy for me to do their work for them. Their energy is with them for a purpose. To pass their negativity onto someone else deprives them of learning how to remove it. This is similar to a caregiver doing everything for a child, and the child does not learn to manage on their own. I was shown a scene where a baby was carried up the stairs by her care-giver. As time went on and the child grew older, the caregiver was still carrying the child up the stairs, so the child never learned to climb the stairs on her own.

I see many empathic clients in my Intuitive Life Coaching practice who absorb negativity from others so I give them this method to follow. I also use this method for global events that I sense even though I don't know mentally what is happening or where it is. I often used to feel upset and out-of-sorts when I absorbed negative energies that were released from people somewhere in the world. Sometimes it would take me half the day to console myself, so that I could deal with the situation. Eventually when I felt clear enough, I would meditate and send loving energy to these people. Now using this new method, I feel the negative energy, but don't let it in, and am immediately ready and able to send much more intense love and healing energy back. I can sense when the love energy enters someone and it helps them in whatever way Creator decides. It is such an amazing feeling to know that you are helping people anywhere in the world. This method is very helpful even in personal situations if someone is angry with me. Instead of buying into their anger energy, I can feel it, but be unaltered by their forceful negativity, and react in a completely loving and kind manner. The one-sided argument has nowhere to go except dissolve. Then the solution to the problem is easily found.

CHAPTER 20

HUMILITY AND PEACE

Humility

I had been asking for a long time for help in becoming one with Spirit; this was the help I received. One morning during my wakening process but still in the drowsiness from a deep sleep, some strong messages surfaced. First I was shown a famous author on a park bench, sitting there for a long time. The message was that he had sat there until he had become humble. Only then was he able to create his book and receive the abundance and fame that followed. I was shown my son being given tunes and lyrics that he would write soon. I was shown other famous song-writers having their soon-to-be songs delivered to them during their sleep. The songs looked as if they were in a spiritual gift box entering their solar plexus chakra. It would be opened when the time was right. Similarly I was shown famous authors and famous and infamous people all over the world receiving what would become their future creations being transported to them. It made me realize that the large majority of people if not all of us rely on Spirit for our creative ideas. It was a very humbling experience.

I was also shown people who used their intellectual genius, physical brawn, emotional drama or spiritual prowess and practices to set them just a bit apart and above the average person. Their egoist misconception is that they developed this level of ability alone, with no help from Creator. This leads to a superiority complex. There was an image of a particular woman who led a workshop that I had recently attended. I was shown that she had an attitude of superiority toward the general population which blocked her from her strive for enlightenment. I had personally felt this woman's struggle within herself and understood that her air of supremacy was really a cover up for her low self-esteem. She was also very masculine in her nature. I was shown that sometimes personality develops from challenges in life that leave a person with a yin/yang imbalance. If an incident from a male influence was the precursor of a person's development of low self-esteem and his or her ensuing awkward development, then the female aspect of the personality would extend for the rescue and vice-versa for the opposite. Either way, humility plays a huge role in healing the superiority/inferiority mind-set. Humility brings gratefulness for all incidents in life and the knowledge that each challenge is necessary for growth. Humble people understand that they are living the Truth, and there is no need for defence and therefore no need for rescue. Humility creates a high self-esteem because it allows your true soul personality to emerge and shine. Soul personality is directly linked to Creator and is worthy, loving and unpretentious.

Still in the half-dream state, I was shown that as a child my self-esteem was quite low. I remembered that my childhood mind had created a fantasy that I would be rescued by someone who would take me far away to a beautiful estate, buy me a pony and lavish unconditional love upon me, and no matter what I did I would not get in trouble. No reflection was intended to my real family, it was just an eight-year-old's imagination! My mind had somehow morphed this childhood desire into a teenage wish to be different and distinct from those around me. I could see this parallel attitude in many other people my age and older as part of the ego identity. This develops into the part of our adult ego personality that keeps us separate from the whole and blocked from being one with All There Is. I was then shown that in order to be one with All, I had to heal my self-esteem. My ego-mind had been falsely bolstering my confidence in the only way it knew how.

In this dream-state, I released all the negativity that had caused my low self-esteem. I could feel my being come into line with Earth and its entire people. I was no longer needy for recognition or acceptance from others or desiring to be just a little bit nicer or a trifle kinder than others were. I could see that I fit into the population of Earth, and my feet felt grounded like they had never felt before. I could see in myself connecting to people from my soul-light at my solar plexus, shining like a flashlight to their solar plexus' and gradually multiplying to all people of Earth eternally shining and glowing. I could see Heaven coming through the veil to Earth and filling all people with light, whereas before it had always been just out of reach for all of us. I felt such a strong vibration of humility being shed upon me that I was overwhelmed with the sensation.

I was shown that teachers and leaders often have the outlook that in order to be successful in getting their ideas across to others, they must have a superior attitude, commanding stance and viewpoint. Otherwise they think people will not listen to them or take them seriously. Then I was shown Jesus and how He was a grass roots leader of people. He had no air of superiority, he was wholly humble. I woke up realizing that there has never been a teacher or person as well received as Jesus. I rest my case on humility!

Peace

Patience is the key to a peaceful life. Living a peaceful

life is the key to unconditional love and joy. The three go hand-in-hand. Peace is attainable temporarily through Focused Breathing and by doing the Mother Earth Visualization. Once you feel absolute serenity, you will want it to be constantly present within you 24 hours a day, seven days a week. Unconditional patience brings with it unconditional peace. No matter what happens during your day if you react to all agitation with a patient attitude you will be living in peace. A patient mind-set helps you to build strong, loving bonds with others. It encourages self-esteem for yourself and others along with kind and lasting relationships.

The way to increase peace in your life is, firstly to declare this intention to your Higher Power. Secondly, identify circumstances in your daily life that trigger you to withdraw from your calm state and enter into an anxious state. Release the trigger with one of the clearing and replenishing methods described in Chapter 14. Once the awareness of the trigger is recognized and released, instead of reacting the usual way when it erupts again, you will be able to respond in a peaceful way. You will find that the trigger has lost its power over you. You may need to clear away deeper layers if you are still reacting. Or you may be pleasantly surprised that incidences that used to propel you into frantic states are now not rendering any negative response in you at all. Many people live their lives in a state of constant stress without realizing it. Nervous tension is the norm to them. Often this occurs because of tenseness in the home where they were raised. Because it is a familiar way of being, they may continue to create new relationships and new situations that contain the same or similar nervous energy. They may bring a sense of anxiousness to their job or have uneasy energy around a group of people at a party, club or gathering. It's often an ingrained, normal feeling to them, not recognizable as a hindrance.

Peace is reliant on having a healthy self-esteem. If someone opposes, criticizes, or attempts to offend you, and you are at peace with yourself, knowing you have done your best, their negativity will fall away from you as water off the back of a duck. When confronted with any obstacle or challenge, or memory of the past, the peace-filled person finds no guilt or remorse within herself nor does she seek to find it in others. Instead, she learns from the situation which improves her likelihood of making better future choices and actions.

CHAPTER 21

RELATIONSHIPS

Channelling from Spirit, recorded July, 2013.
Divine Relationship

"Divine Relationships were primarily designed to bring love into people's lives and to quicken each person's ascent up the ladder of enlightenment. Similar to children in a classroom sharing their show and tell, the couple was to have different experiences, often of opposite nature, and then share these findings thereby reducing the amount of work to half for each person. Reciprocal learning in this manner allows the soul to experience the other's lessons as its own thereby quickening the process of soul-learning for each person. Reciprocal learning is not only for romantic couples, but it also applies to business partnerships, friendships, family relationships, and connection with a pet. There are some necessary ingredients for this type of soul learning to take place. Divine Relationships include the following aspects.

-There must be mutual respect and compassion.

-Both must be living in an environment of love, not necessarily in love, but certainly not living in a place of negativity or fear.

-Each person is responsible for himself and to the other.

-Each has balanced male/female personalities as much as possible.

-No one person is in control of the other, and no manipulation or abusive traits are initiated or tolerated.

-Each person gives to the other with the attitude of loving kindness as opposed to giving with the attitude of sacrifice.

-During any problems or disagreements, each person is listened to and has equal input.

-Decisions are made through compromise and are agreeable to each person.

-Judgment is not any part of a Divine relationship. Openness and allowing of differences in each personality is accepted. If it is a parent/child relationship obviously there will be times when discipline is required. This discipline is to be given in a kind and loving but firm way designed to enhance the individuality of the child, and allow her differences to be accepted.

Karmic Relationship

The second type of relationship we will discuss is the Karmic Relationship. Again this includes romantic couples, business partnerships, friends, relatives, and pets. People often come to this lifetime with a low vibration caused by taking part in wars, greed, ethnic cleansing, and all negative/dark activities from past and present lives. Through these events and countless others, many people have gathered for themselves much negative karma that needs to be released. All karma must be released for a soul to become one with its Higher Power. The karmic relationship is available for souls to partake in, as these liaisons result in each partner releasing much of their karmic debt. Basically each person in the relationship is paying his or her karmic debt not only to the partner but to the partner's soul group and to the Whole. Some ways karmic debt is released:

-Positive energy shown toward another, especially during conflict.

-Being a care-giver for another who is in ill health or has some form of dis-ease.

-Raising children.

-Helping others: strangers or known.

-Caring for elderly or dying people especially parents and children.

-Working in an environment of service to others.

-Being a caregiver to people, animals, vegetation, marine life, Mother Earth and all of her inhabitants.

-Projecting a loving attitude to all who you encounter.

-Meditating with a loving attitude.

-Continuing within a relationship until the karmic release is finished, (but not to the detriment of your being.)

-Bravely enduring an illness, temporary or terminal, and gratefully allowing others to attend to your needs that you are unable to perform.

-Living a conscious life with the purpose of mindfulness for all others in the pursuit of oneness with all."

Excerpt from my *On Wings of Love* Newsletter, *"Harmonize Your Relationships"* April, 2012

"What is the purpose of having relationships anyway? They can be so wonderful and rewarding at times, and so challenging at other times. They can be full of soul-nurturing love, or can be like an emotional roller coaster. Relationships can take you to the highest of highs, the lowest of lows, or anywhere in between. They can be full of joy or full of pain, and most likely a combination of all of the above.

So why are we compelled to engage in relationships time after time, knowing that there will be pain involved at some point during the liaison and almost certainly at the end of it? One way to reunite with Spirit is through relationships. When you learn to love another being, you are creating and enhancing the tools you need to have a more perfect relationship with Spirit.

Monks and nuns and people who live similar singular lifestyles believe that the only way or perhaps the best and quickest way to reunite with Spirit is through a path solely devoted to God. They believe that focusing all their attention on God throughout their days will bring them to a more enlightened status in the eyes of Spirit. I believe that both methods are equal in value. Both have many challenges that need to be overcome, and both have large spiritual growth potential. For each method, sometimes growth is realized, and sometimes not.

Children learn how to relate to parents, siblings, peers, teachers, neighbours, pets and others, which teaches them how to create and maintain adult relationships. As adults, we learn how to relate to our spouse, children, friends, boss, employees and acquaintances, which teaches us how to recreate and remember our relationship with Spirit.

Ideally in childhood, we discover the pitfalls and learn to navigate around the obstacles that cause tension in relationships. If we learn this well, we have less challenging relationships as adults because firstly, we learn to choose friends who are compatible with us. Secondly, we learn how to relate to others in a helpful, non-offending manner and to overlook mildly upsetting behaviours.

You are half of the relationship. You cannot fix or change anyone else; you can only change yourself. Each person is responsible for his/her own behaviour. Becoming a better you will automatically make you a better partner. You will create a relationship environment that is easier and more joyful for you to maintain. You can be a good example to others, and your new improved energy will emanate through those who are close to you. This gives them the opportunity to rise up and follow. How wonderful it is to experience yourself and your loved ones expanding your horizons!"

As you change and grow, people around you will start to notice. Your energy alters and if they are motivated to remain in your life, they will also choose to change for the better. This adjustment is often unconscious at first, but will eventually expand to include the conscious mind. If people are not willing to grow spiritually, they may choose to distance themselves from you. As you flourish, you will attract people of like-mindedness into your circle of friends, for that is the Law of Attraction.

Ask not what your relationships can do for you, but instead, what you can do for your relationships! Below are some exercises you can do to increase positive feelings even in your most challenging relationships. There is a meditation that helps to create a positive atmosphere for meeting new people and it also works for your existing relationships. This projects a light and positive energy into these encounters. Dissolving an angry or argumentative situation and infusing it with kindness and understanding will also be addressed.

EXERCISES

These exercises as with all the other exercises in this book are designed to heal with love energy. It is only offered to the person, never imposed upon them. You may find that your energy is rejected by them or that it has not been absorbed well. If this is the case, you may try again later with a more gentle approach, meaning with decreased energy output that may be more compatible and acceptable. It is important to bring love into yourself after these exercises so you are left energized and full of light.

Projecting Love Energy to an Unknown Person

This exercise is used for easing into a new relationship with someone you have not yet met. It helps the relationship

start off with positive energy. It could be used for a job inter-
view, a roommate in college, a co-worker, pet sitting, babysit-
ting or for the family or friends of a new partner. There are
many applications that it can be used for. I do this visualization
from the third person perspective, although you may choose
to practice it from first person.

Take a few Focused Breaths and ask your angels for
help.

Third person perspective: Visualize yourself in your
aura standing a few feet away from where you are sitting.
See the light and beautiful energy that you possess swirling
around your aura getting stronger and more loving and powerful.

Now see the person you will soon be meeting standing
in her aura about ten feet away from where you see yourself
in your aura. See her energy swirling around her. If you know
what she looks like, you may incorporate that into the vision.
If not, but you know her name; put a generic woman into the
aura with her name tag pinned to her shirt. If you don't know
her name or what her appearance is, simply envision a generic
person with the intention of, "the person who I will be meeting." Be as specific as possible, for instance: "the person who
will be interviewing me on Saturday morning", or "the person
I am to meet at the airport on Wednesday afternoon" or "the
roommate with whom I will be living in September."

Envision both of you taking some steps forward until
you are standing about three feet apart. Visualize the energy
from both of your auras mixing together and swirling around.
See both of you smiling and enjoying the visit. Feel relaxed
and happy and that you are getting along very well.

Continue for a couple of minutes then finish the
visualization. When the physical meeting occurs, you may

feel as though you have met before. This eliminates or at least lessens the awkwardness of meeting a complete stranger, and the meeting will have the best possible outcome for all.

Projecting Love Energy to a Known Person

This exercise is used for close relationships: children, parents, spouses, siblings and partners. It is good when you are getting together with a loved one who you haven't seen for a while. You may only have a short time to connect, so you want to be comfortable and on the same page so you don't waste precious time getting re-acquainted with one another. It also puts all negative energy from past events into the background and allows the souls to connect in a deeper and more authentic manner.

Start with a few Focused Breaths and ask your angels for help.

Similar to the exercise above, envision yourself in your aura and your loved one in her aura facing you. Step closer and move into each other's aura. See the love energy swirling around absorbing into her. When I do this I feel negative energy draining from my loved one into Mother Earth. Once this drainage has been completed, swirl the love energy for another minute or so. Each person is left with a melding of energy. This exchange of energy dissipates back to each person's natural state after the meeting is finished. Remember to notice how amazing the meeting is and how it is wonderfully different from other times you have met this person.

Infusing Love into Challenging Relationships

This exercise is used for improving challenging relationships. It is used for bringing love into a person who has seemingly little love for you or for others. A person such as this needs love to heal her heart and her emotions. Love is projected into the general vicinity of where the person lives. If the person is very negative she may not be able to absorb love energy while awake, so it is sent to her home or a room where she will be relaxed. Her heart and soul can absorb the love vibration while her resistant mind is calm. She can absorb it if and when her subconscious mind chooses to. It may take several times doing this exercise before you notice a change in the attitude of the person you are trying to heal.

Take a few Focused Breaths.

Have the intention of sending love to the challenging person. If you know where her home is, then visualize it. If not, then just have the intent of filling her place with love and light.

Generate within your heart the feeling of cuddling an infant or embracing a favourite child or pet. Feel this love energy expanding as much as possible. Again visualize the home or person that you are sending the energy to. Project the love energy forward into the desired location. This can be accomplished by several methods.

a) Visualize your love energy all around you as large ball of light. Deliver this light to the location by seeing your angels take it there.

b) Visualize a large hand picking it up from you and transporting it to the location.

c) See and feel your energy streaming from you to the location as a garden hose carrying the light and spraying it into the room.

Use your imagination. I generally envision the room first and fill it with light.

I have done this a number of times each resulting in a much warmer rapport with the person.

CHAPTER 22

ONENESS

Oneness is to be in harmony with your Higher Power and with all people and with all beings and with Earth herself. When we all learn to consistently love All There Is, life will be peaceful with good will toward everyone and everything that encompasses Earth.

What are the necessary steps to achieve this goal of Oneness?

Oneness means leaving the world of duality behind and moving forward into the world of Oneness. Oneness is living one's existence in harmony with the soul. It embraces love, positivity, joy, peace, tranquillity, forgiveness, acceptance, helpfulness and all good things. Duality is a combination of the soul and the ego usually in equal doses. The ego is consistent with negativity and fear in all forms such as racism, hate, meanness, abusiveness, anger, selfishness, and so forth.

An important thing to remember is that the intention to change and grow in spirituality produces an underlying forward motion. Higher Power has such a potent omnipresence that for those people who choose to follow their soul path, the urgency and the power of the pull seems impossible to deny. This pull manifests from gut feelings such as intuition, a deep knowing, confirmation goose bumps, synchronicities, and messages. This pull is not willing to be ignored. It is present for very compelling and persuasive reasons: it is why many people have come to Earth at this time for purposes of spiritual growth and remembering their soul's objectives.

Forward motion includes attaining a wealth of knowledge instigated by a series of instances specifically designed for an individual to learn or remember who they truly are. Some situations are created to envelope the person in their own negativity so blatantly obvious that it requires attention. Once apparent, this negativity can be removed and replaced with love vibration which advances one toward the completion of their soul journey.

Often during the journey to Oneness an individual is asked if they are ready to move forward into the next level of enlightenment. It usually manifests as a feeling of stagnancy, or perhaps that one is going around in circles. This is the time to do the "Door Visualization" illustrated below. This enables the power of the directive: "Ask and you shall receive." This is the way Spirit works in a quiet unassuming role abiding by the Universal Laws. Each person is responsible for their own journey and for the swiftness for which it progresses. Spirit is always available to help when asked.

Adherence to inner peace leads to correct choices. Whenever a difficult decision is impending, engaging the inner awareness is essential. Implementing "Peace Evaluation", which is one of the exercises below, will help to weigh each element to be examined and derive a verdict most compatible with the soul purpose. When inner peace is compromised from feelings of unhappiness, anxiety, being out of sorts and apathy, then ill health may emerge. These sensations and emotions and illnesses are intended to encourage further analysis of life circumstances in order to evolve positive change. Eventually all negativity will be accounted for and urged to be discharged, which then expands the accumulation of light. Climbing the ladder of enlightenment is directly proportional to the amount of positivity and light gained within.

EXERCISES

Doorway Visualization

This visualization is used whenever you are feeling spiritually stagnant, or bored, and that you are not moving forward.

Take some Focused Breaths and ask your angels for help. Count down from 10 to 1 with the intent of going deeper into a meditative state.

Visualize a door in front of you. Use your imagination; the more real you make it the better it works. I usually see a door made of white light with a gold door knob. Write on the door what it is that you are manifesting. For instance:

{Insert your name}'s Door to Unconditional Love

{Insert your name}'s Door to Enlightenment

{Insert your name}'s Door to Peace

Next, intend that when you go through the door, you leave everything behind that you don't need anymore. You may want to say goodbye or just wave as you go. Let your angels decide who and what will come with you, and who and what will remain behind. They can see what you need from the big picture much better than what you can see from your tunnel vision that is available to earthlings.

Move toward the door and put your hand on the door knob. Read the sign on the door one more time and say out loud your version of the following: "I now go through this door that says (fill in the blank) and I take with me only that which I need. I leave all else behind with gratefulness and love.

Walk through the door and close it behind you. All others who are meant to be with you on the new leg of your journey will be accompanying you. You may not see them, but you will probably feel the warmth of their energy beside you. Stand for a few breaths and feel your new surroundings.

Look down and in front of your feet is a path made of white light. When you are ready, step onto the path and start walking forward. You may meet light beings along the way, or you may see a green meadow or serene lake or whatever brings you joy. You may want to relax for a while as you absorb this beautiful new vibration. Soon you will want to continue walking up your path for as long as you like, noticing what happens along the way.

When you are ready, count from 1 to 10 to bring yourself back to your normal conscious state.

Peaceful Choices

Think of the choices for a decision you need to make. It may be a choice between two jobs, or making a large purchase perhaps a house or car. It may be deciding whether to engage in a new relationship, join a group or association, move to a different city, or apply for college. Be unemotional or think of yourself as a fly-on-the-wall.

Take a few Focused Breaths and ask your angels for help. Count down from 10 to 1.

Consider the choices you have to choose from and develop a visual for each one. Try to make the visual as accurate and real as possible. Then envision yourself as you would be in the future had you selected choice number one. See and hear what is happening. Notice your perceptions and your mood. Trust your angels to bring to you the feelings and sensations that would be surrounding you in this choice. Sit with this energy for a while. Does it feel peaceful? Is it a good feeling? Are you happy? How is your inner being or soul reacting to the stimuli you are giving it? It may help for you to rate this feeling from 1 to 10, 1 depicting a lousy feeling and 10 being a great feeling. When you have had ample time to review your emotions in this state, release it, but stay in your meditative state.

Next, see yourself in the future had you selected choice number two. Give it the same consideration as choice number one. Ask the same questions as above and give these feelings a rating from 1 to 10. When you have had enough time to evaluate this option, count yourself back to normal consciousness. Trust that you have been given all the information and the intuition that you need to make a decision that is harmonious to your soul. You may need to repeat this exercise a few times for important or potentially life-changing decisions before you feel a firm and consistent selection is achieved.

CHAPTER 23

DIVINE MOTHER

Divine Mother channelled through me early in the spring of 2011 with the message that she would soon be able to spread her nurturing energy throughout the world. There were many things on earth that required change including the spiritual vibration of earthlings which she said had to rise much higher; the feminine energy needed to increase dramatically and it was vital for people to embrace love and release hate and negativity. The general populace was required to become more giving, compassionate and kind.

Since then, Divine Mother energy has been steadily increasing. She comes to me often, especially in the mornings just as I am waking. She fills me with her love and compassion for all of Earth and its inhabitants. I feel as if I am glowing as she imparts her energy upon me. How grateful I am for our connection. Recently Divine Mother has informed me that I am to help her bring her energy to Earth in her augmented and astounding ways. I am to inform people of her strong presence and that she is a powerful one to pray to. She deeply loves all people. She advises women to be kind and understanding and patient with their counterpart males, as they have chosen to live this life in a very challenging time. Earth is changing from male energy dominance to female energy of compassion and understanding. It is easier to exist in this feminine authority if you are female. She blesses all the men who have the courage and conviction to live here under these circumstances. Help them to embrace their feminine aspects so they can become balanced and move forward in their spiritual journey.

Divine Mother guides me often during readings and healings, filling the client with whatever energy is necessary to heal emotionally, mentally and physically and to grow spiritually. She will present herself to me just before a client arrives for a reading and inform me that she will be performing the reading through me. Mother's energy is very light and comforting as well as strong and healing.

Divine Mother attended my workshops and performed group healings. She showed me how she wanted to perform her task and advised me what to say and do. Near the end of the spiritual meetings she directed me to ask permission from the participants for her to heal them. Naturally they all agreed. I was guided to put everyone into a light meditation during which she presented each member of the group with specific healing energy for their highest good. I saw her light being standing in front of each person for a few seconds as she proceeded around the room. I could feel her powerful energy penetrating into the participants. Some of the things that were delivered were confidence, love, clarity, release from emotional upset, motivation to get a job, and many more. At one point I could see Mother shooting light into a participant's knee, and the knee lighting up brightly. Divine Mother informed me of what it was that she was giving each person so I could relate that to them after the healing. As I delivered the information that she had given me, each person nodded and agreed that they had needed that particular healing energy. The person with the knee issue said it felt much better. Some people said they felt her presence filling them with love, peace and joy. Others said they just felt happy, more complete.

Next, Divine Mother said she wanted to bless the water that each person had brought with them. We put all the bottles in the centre of the room and again went into a light meditative state. Divine Mother blessed each person's water bottle with healing energy specific to that person. The directions given with the healing water was the following. Each time we wanted to drink from the bottle, we were to hug the water to our heart and fill it with our love energy for a few seconds. Take a breath for the void which allowed for new healing energy to be inserted into the water. We were to take a few sips, until we were no longer thirsty. Mother said sending love into the water would put the vibration of what needed to be cured into the water so she could attend to it specifically. Once healed from that issue, the subsequent love energy we put into the water would restart the process for the next most important health issue to be rectified. We were able to refill the bottles multiple times with the Divine healing energy remaining, as long as there was even one drop of water left in the bottle from the original water blessing. The workshop participants told me they felt tingling energy running through their bodies when they drank from the bottles and that they felt happier. I too felt this healing energy.

CHAPTER 24

EARTH CHANGES

Channellings from Spirit recorded May, 2014

"This Earth journey that you have agreed to undertake is happening during the most important time in history. Time is moving very quickly now, and will continue to speed up for the next few years. Now Earth dwellers can gain quickened ascent into spiritual realms that in the past centuries would have taken 20 or more lifetimes to complete. Welcome these Earth changes and allow yourself to move forward with the ebb and flow of the Universe. We hope and pray that the vast majority of people will see and move into the Light. Earth is now changing into a planet where only light beings will survive. All those of darkness and negativity will either transmute their darkness into light, or they will be encouraged to find other living accommodations.

Looking ahead in time, we see many changes occurring on Earth, and in mankind. We see Earth being covered with increasing intensity of light to the point where it is again returned to the original paradise. Some will see it as the Garden of Eden or Heaven on Earth. This is the reason why so many Light Beings are having human lives today. They are here not only to witness the changes, but also to help others who have decided to be a part of Earth's Ascension. All those who choose to ascend have already been assigned to Light Workers who will give them the necessary tools to move forward in their spirituality.

All who entered Earth for this lifetime have been screened very carefully. All who are here have come with a strong purpose. They have already chosen either to ascend, or to not ascend. Many of those who have chosen not ascend but wanted to be part of this miraculous process have come as helpers. They have come to be a spring board for those who are ascending. What we mean by this, is that the majority of the helpers have not yet developed the vibration necessary to ascend themselves. Instead, they are contributing to the ascension by helping those who are ready. Often the helpers are a negative influence in a light person's life. Negative influence propels the light person to strive for and achieve a higher level of spirituality, strength of character, and a powerful conviction to search for and find more light. Only from experiencing the negative, can the positive be recognized and amplified. We are blessing all of you who have come to Earth at this time. Be grateful to negative people around you, as they are here for important and valid reasons.

When you have the tools to help you, your journey becomes much faster and more rewarding. There is much for you all to do, and this is only the beginning. When you are drawn to a book, movie, program, workshop or other such modes of gaining information, follow that intuition and learn what is being brought forward for you to learn. There is always enough time, but time is limited. This sounds like a contrasting statement, but what we mean is that you will always have enough time to pursue your spirituality by moving forward at a sufficient speed. If you dilly dally, and procrastinate, you will find that you are pushed to move forward and it may feel a little uncomfortable. It is with great hope that we close the chapters of this book. We are all of the opinion that those who follow their hearts and souls will find salvation in this lifetime."

Creating Heaven on Earth

Channelling from Spirit, recorded Sept, 2014

"What is the point of working so hard to become enlightened? It is to live a life of bliss and joy. The information in this book is just the beginning; there is much more spiritual advancement available for all those who seek it. The creation of Heaven on Earth on a large scale is possible now for the second time in the history of Earth. After following the instructions in this book, there are several steps to creating Heaven on Earth.

Your Higher Self will be sure that you are ready for this way of life and are able to manifest all that is good. All things that are beautiful and that help you to continue to grow on your spiritual journey to enlightenment will become available to you. That is what Heaven on Earth is; the perfect environment to propel you into the higher realms of enlightenment.

Beyond the present human world lies a reality filled with so much bliss and love. This is to be attained for all those who choose it and actively seek it.

Earth will become a world of positivity. There will be enough food for all. Everyone who chooses to be healthy will be so. All those who want to work will have perfect jobs that are enjoyable and satisfying. The world will change to a lush and beautiful place where all good things are possible. Personal relationships will flourish in loving ways, and there will be abundance of all good things. People will project good will toward all others. People will not age as quickly or at least as they do now, and will live for as long as they choose to.

Divine presence is now on Earth and will continue to expand and fill all those who invite it in. Do you want to be part of this amazing journey of ascension? Everyone who has the serious intention of ascending will be invited to come along.

245

What do you need to do to show serious intent of ascending? It is imperative that you follow your heart, your guidance and your Higher Power. It is just as simple as that. If you allow yourself to move in a spiritually forward motion, you will be able to digest the information gathered here in this book. You will become more highly attuned to your Soul Path and you will be given the information on how to acquire for yourself a place in Heaven on Earth."

The angels' purpose for me writing this book is to spread the words, intentions and vibrations of the angelic realm to as many people as possible. The sooner the majority of the population on Earth has the intention to move forward on their spiritual path, the sooner Earth will journey to become a heavenly place to live. We can truly create Heaven on Earth, in our own homes, and then spread it far and wide, covering the whole Earth, generating peace, love and joy to all, and contributing to the Universe in a positive way. I am receiving channellings and information to write a second book designed to help people create Heaven on Earth. May you always be blessed with Universal Light, Love and joy forever. Amen.

THE END

WHICH TRULY IS THE BEGINNING!

EXERCISE LIST

Jill Michelle heard messages from angels when she was a young child. She lost the ability for a while, but after a life-threatening accident, she became wide awake to the spiritual realm. After honing her skills of communication, Spirit guided her to write this book and channelled divine wisdom through her to share with readers. Jill facilitates workshops and performs Angel readings and Intuitive Life Coaching sessions over the phone and video calls for clients internationally. Please see her website for more information.

www.jillmichelle.ca

jillmichelle.ca@gmail.com

61451824R00143

Made in the USA
Charleston, SC
23 September 2016